The BIG

To Anne
Enjoy the Ride

How to Survive the Rollercoaster Ride of Business Ownership

Kevin Stansfield

Printed in the United Kingdom

Illustrations by Emma Paxton, Imagistic
Imagistic.co.uk

First Printing, 2017

ISBN 978-0-9957390-6-2 (Paperback)
ISBN 978-0-9957390-7-9 (eBook)

Librotas Books
Portsmouth, Hampshire
PO2 9NT

www.LibrotasBooks.com

Contents

The BIG Foreword

Ten years ago, I had the pleasure of meeting Kevin Stansfield following my on-stage presentation in the UK, talking to an audience of budding entrepreneurs about the perks and pitfalls of being in business for oneself, and how it takes a certain *type* of individual to successfully handle the ups and downs of business ownership. Like me and Kevin, true entrepreneurs have an affinity for business ownership – an almost innate desire to build something great and a passion for a purpose greater than us.

As a multi-millionaire entrepreneur and the owner of the No. 1 business coaching firm in the world (*Entrepreneur* magazine), ActionCOACH Global, I am proud that Kevin became one of the most award-winning ActionCOACH business coaches in the UK, and, like me, found his passion in guiding other business owners to success – some almost out of the depths of despair.

We *understand* those 'rollercoaster' moments when people sometimes feel like giving up – and some do – but after starting up over 30 successful businesses, there is a certain 'never say die' attitude that I learned to live by during my own journey in business ownership.

It is fantastic that Kevin is now parlaying his 10 years of expertise as a veteran business coach, plus his natural affinity for the business owner's journey, into a book like *The Big Dipper: How to Survive the Rollercoaster Ride of Business Ownership*. The lessons Kevin teaches through his fictional characters in *The Big Dipper* are invaluable to anyone on that bumpy ride of business ownership. *The Big Dipper* not only entertains as it educates, it inspires anyone who might be struggling in their entrepreneurial endeavours to take the right and necessary steps to win.

I highly endorse Kevin, as both a business coach and the author of *The Big Dipper*. When business owners read *The Big Dipper*, they will undoubtedly relate to many of the situations Ken encounters, as a father who owns a business that needs some help to not just survive, but thrive. They will undoubtedly also relate to Ken and his dilemmas, and benefit, as Ken does, from the mentorship of a kind and successful entrepreneur he meets by chance, and others he meets on his journey.

The scientific basis behind why things happen the way they do, in both business and human nature, as well as many of the lessons interlaced within the pages of *The Big Dipper*, and also the fictional account of a business owner who could be any of us at one time or another in our entrepreneurial careers, make Kevin's book required reading for anyone running or even thinking of starting their own business.

Kevin definitely subscribes, as a fellow business coach, entrepreneur, and now author, to my life vision of 'World Abundance through Business Re-education'. He not only has the passion and the heart to be a business owner, he helps business owners with his dynamic coaching techniques, and, now, in his writing.

Cheers, Kevin!

Brad Sugars
Founder & Chairman, ActionCOACH Global

The BIG
Introduction

There were many reasons to write this book. To prove to myself that I could do it, to pass on over 20 years of knowledge learnt from my own, my clients' and some of the best business speakers' and writers' experiences, but the main reason is to help as many business owners as I can to avoid the fate that befell the person to whom this book is dedicated:

My late father Kenneth Henry Stansfield (1942–2008).

In the eyes of their sons, most fathers are gods. They are the figure-head of the family, the protector and, at least to a certain age, they are invincible.

My father was exactly that to me. A very successful accountant, who did in fact buy a business off a man in a pub and who went on to grow that business during the entrepreneurial boom of Margaret Thatcher's 1980s.

Nobody really knew what went on inside my father's head apart from him. He was a very proud man and to show any sign of weakness was not the done thing. Whatever challenge came up he went at it, head on and with the blind faith that it would be alright in the end.

This thinking served him very well for many years until the recession of the early 1990s, when his one-size-fits-all approach did not fit anymore.

However, as a family we did not know there was a problem until much later, in fact until it was too late. So proud was my father that he took the full burden of the business on his shoulders and never said a word. He became grumpier, more stressed, the holidays and spending got less, but at no point did he say anything was wrong or ask for help.

Until one day, when he opened up that the business was losing money and the bank would no longer support him with more. By then I had left home to seek my own accountancy career and was fortunate enough to have some colleagues who could help him to a certain extent. But by then it was damage limitation. The best he could do was hand the business over and walk away from as much debt as he could.

My father was 55 at the time, not much older than I am now. Apart from a few part-time jobs he never worked again. His health deteriorated, and he finally passed away at the age of 65, only just making pension age.

Unfortunately he will never get to read this book. That in itself is testament to the message I hope that you get from the book, namely that life is short. If you don't plan out what you want to achieve, you may well find you run out of time to do it.

I hope that you find this book unlike most of the books that you have ever read before. It has been laid out specifically to help as many people as I can. Some people will love stories, some will enjoy the science and detail, and others will just want to get to the point and move on.

Each chapter is divided into three parts. The first is the story of Ken, my father, well sort of. Ken is actually a combination of many of the business owners I have coached over the years, some good and some bad, but each with challenges that they have had to overcome to become a successful businessman or woman.

The second part is the lesson I wish my father had learnt, and I would like you to learn, as to why certain things happen in business and in life. Just remember that you are very unlikely to be the first person to encounter a challenge in your life, and the more lessons you learn, the more prepared you will be when they happen again.

The third part is the BIG Action that I recommend you take. Think of these as your safety restraint that will keep you safe during the ups and downs of your rollercoaster journey.

As for Ken, I want him to resonate with as many people as possible. No matter where you started in life, whether you are male, female, old or young, Ken represents all business people who get into business in search of a better life for themselves and their families, but get carried away on the 'rollercoaster'. If they do not seek out help along the way, they are destined to stay on that rollercoaster, or worse, come crashing off way before the ride has ended, as was the case for my father.

I have used the names of family and friends, and if you are one of them and read this, I hope you realise that the characters are not a representation of you, unless of course you like them.

I dearly hope that you read the whole book, resonate with Ken's journey, and learn the lessons that I wish my father could have learnt. I hope you put them into practice so that you and your family can benefit from the successes that owning and running your own business can bring.

Oh and if you need any help, please, please, please, don't put your head in the sand; give me, any of our coaches or just anybody who will listen, a call, and let us help you safely reach your goals and enjoy the ride to them.

Until then, happy reading.

The BIG Job

Ken was an ordinary guy, with an ordinary job, drove an ordinary car, had an ordinary family, lived in an ordinary house, in an ordinary street, in an ordinary town. There was nothing special about Ken; you would pass him in the street without a second glance.

The only real thing that made Ken stand out from the crowd was that he had a rather less than ordinary job. Ken was the finance director of one of the largest companies in the town. He had worked all his life at this job. He studied hard at school, got the required exams to get him into university, where he again studied hard to get his degree, and then got a job with a local accountancy firm. He worked his way up through the ranks, gaining promotions, until his dream job appeared in the local newspaper.

Ken was 35 when the job came up and he was in the prime of his professional life. His track record put him in the perfect position to get the job and so it was no surprise to him or his close friends and family that he got it.

So here he was 10 years later, in his dream office, with his dream desk, looking out of a picture window over the town which he loved to bits. It was Friday afternoon and he was due to leave on holiday that evening, taking his family to Disney World for a two-week summer holiday.

Ken should have been one of the happiest guys alive. He had it all, well everything he had ever dreamed of, but he was far from happy; in fact if you had been a fly on the wall looking at him you would have sworn that he was about to jump out the window. So what was wrong?

As Ken reminisced on the last 10 years in his perfect job, he could see three distinct phases he had gone through.

The first four years it was the excitement of the new role and the growth that the company had gone through. Learning about the company, coming up with new ideas and being allowed to implement these and see changes.

The next four years was the consolidation of these changes, bringing on the team and implementing systems and processes, so that they could do the work and not be reliant on him and the other directors. As a result, the company was able to grow more quickly and more profitably than it had done before.

The third phase was the choice phase which he had been in for the last couple of years, where he had not taken any action. Although the company was successful, it was now such a size that anything that needed changing took far too long to happen. He had trained his team so well that they just got on with the job and his input was rarely asked for. Finally and probably the most influential fact was that the managing director who had hired him 10 years ago had recently retired. His replacement was, in Ken's opinion, not half the man of his predecessor. In fact, on many occasions Ken actually thought he was a complete idiot. All of this had left Ken somewhat disillusioned about his dream job.

Over the last year, many options had come into his mind. He could look for a new job, which would give him a new challenge, but most of the positions were out of town, which would mean moving the family – and what could beat what he had already done?

He could try and get on better with the new MD and work with him to help move the business forward, but in two years he had seen no signs of the MD wanting to work with him, and is it possible to work with somebody you think is an idiot?

He could start his own business, but what should he do? His skill was in accounts, so a natural move would be to start an account-ancy firm, but he had been in industry so long that trying to get back to general practice just seemed to be too much. He could set up a business to compete with the one he was in, but he was just the finance director and the industry was so technical that it would take to many years to build something that could challenge it. Or he could buy an established business and rely on his business skills to run it, but surely he needed some skill in the business he was to run.

However, the biggest thing holding him back was the fact that his current role was so comfortable. Why would he put his pay, holidays, benefits, and office at risk, just because he was not happy? After all, he had a family to think about.

It was this thought that brought him back to reality with a thump. The clock was showing 5pm and he had to get home to pack for an early flight to Florida in the morning.

Lesson 1
Change is good

Ken's dilemma is a very common one for successful people. The more we have, the more we have to lose. So our appetite for risk reduces and our resistance to change increases.

This is why many millionaires started with nothing, whilst second generation wealthy people do nothing with their wealth, often losing it.

The problem is that we get into a comfort zone with our work and stop taking risks. As a result we can get bored and complacent; we stop learning and thus stop growing. After time it also increases our fear of change, and because it has been so long since we took a risk, we are not used to it, so we get further and further away from reaching our true potential.

The comfort zone diagram summarises what is happening nicely. Our subconscious brain is protecting us from being in the danger zone, as this is where we push ourselves too far, and the risk far outweighs the reward. Yet there is a stage between the danger zone and the comfort zone where we feel most alive, where we are performing at a level above our norm, and where we are learning and growing the most. This is what most people crave and it is definitely what Ken is missing in his life right now.

So how do we overcome this resistance to change? Well, the first thing we have to realise is that we have this resistance, and it is there to protect us. We also have to realise that it may be kicking in too soon, when actually there is relatively little danger there.

If we use the rollercoaster analogy, if there was an actual risk of harm on a rollercoaster, then our fear would be justified, and nobody would ever ride one. So we have to convince ourselves that we are safe. We have to visualise a positive outcome of being on the ride and the excitement of sharing the adventure with friends.

This way of overcoming our resistance to change is depicted in David Gleicher's formula for change, which he devised in the 1960s. My favourite take on it is as follows:

$$(D \times V) + F > R$$

R is a person's resistance to change, or the cost of change.

F is the first steps to make the change.

D is the dissatisfaction of where you are right now.

V is the vision of where you will be when change has happened.

Let me put this into the analogy of the rollercoaster. It is clear that if we have a resistance to riding the biggest rollercoaster in the theme park, knowing that the first steps to get on it, i.e. buy a ticket, queue up and get on, are clearly not enough to make us get on it. What we have to think about is how dissatisfied we are with our current position of not having ridden it. Things like: What will my friends say? What a waste of a ticket to come all this way. Then we have to be engaged with our vision of how we will feel once we have ridden it. This may include the stories we can tell our friends, the adrenaline rush, and the sense of achievement of having ridden it.

In Ken's case, although he is not dissatisfied with his life, he has no real vision of the person he wants to become, and he has no idea on the first steps he needs to take to move forwards.

He therefore has an internal battle going on, with one side craving the excitement of change and the other side wanting the stability of the status quo. Just like someone deciding whether they want to ride the rollercoaster or not.

Fortunately for Ken, he is about to get a little help on both of these from an unexpected encounter...

BIG Actions

1. Review your life at least once a year and decide which of the three phases you are in: growth, consolidate or choices, and be clear on your vision and dissatisfaction.

2. Avoid staying too long in your comfort zone and building up resistance by constantly pushing the edges. Take up a new hobby, try new things; they don't have to be risky, just a little uncomfortable.

3. Challenge those around you to do the same or seek out people who like change. If nobody else is changing, it is hard to be the odd one out. It's no fun being on the rollercoaster on your own!

The BIG Man

Florida in August is a hot and steamy affair, and with two pre-teen kids running and screaming around Disney World, Ken's holiday was becoming far from relaxing. Added to this, he was finding it hard to focus on his family because his mind kept on wandering back to his dissatisfaction at work.

During one tropical storm Ken told his family that he was going to shelter in the cocktail bar and have a beer to think about his future, whilst they went to the Wet and Wild Water Park. As the barman squeezed the lime into the neck of his Corona, a very tall, cool looking gentleman, with a watch that sparkled like a glitter ball, sat on the bar stool next to him. "G'day mate," he said in a clear Australian drawl, "I'll have what he's having."

Ken was not a small man, but this guy was a good five inches taller. He had an aura that was as big as his watch. "Cheers." Ken offered up his bottle and there was a chink of glass on glass. Ken had never been good at small talk; all that training for his accountancy exams had made him more introverted than he was as a kid. But he was on holiday, in a bar on his own, and the only conversation he was having in his head was driving him mad.

"Which part of Oz are you from?" he asked.

The big guy gave a wry smile: "Brissy originally but Vegas for the last 10 years." This made sense to Ken. This guy would fit into the glitz and glamour of Vegas far better than any other city on the planet.

"On holiday with family?" Ken was really digging deep for questions to ask, and he was worried that this was as good as it was going to get.

"Yeah two girls, off in the water park with their mum, not my scene so I thought I would grab a cold one and take a breather." The big guy took a slug of beer, smacked his lips and put the bottle down with a thump.

"Guess you are from England, south coast I reckon, work in some form of professional capacity and from the look on your face when I walked in you are not enjoying it anymore."

Ken was shocked. There he was struggling to ask some nice simple questions to break the ice and this guy had psychoanalysed him in two minutes flat, and slapped him round the face with the reality that he had been struggling with for over two years.

"Errr, yes to most of that," Ken stuttered, trying not to show he was amazed. "What gave it away?"

"I travel a lot, so accents are a bit of a game for me. If you come from the south of England, then there is a higher percentage of middle-aged males in some form of service sector and your hands back this up, whilst your branded but understated clothes suggest a higher than average level of income in a rather restrained profession such as accountancy or legal, and I would now guess accountancy because your eye twitched when I said that word. I had thought that you might be a business owner at one point, but I just did not get a feel for it, probably because I see so many I tend to know them when I see them." The big guy talked very fast and confidently, sipping his beer between sentences.

"Wow, you're good at this, what line of business are you in that makes this so easy for you?" Ken swivelled on his bar stool so that he was now facing the big guy directly.

"I used to buy, build and sell businesses, so I have worked in and around virtually every business there is and have got to know different people styles."

"Used to?" Ken probed.

"Yeah, sort of semi-retired now, trying to be a good dad and spend as much time as I can with the kids. All the businesses I own work without me, so I get to do what is important."

Ken was even more impressed. This guy looked like he was in his early 30s, retired and, by the look of his watch, rather wealthy. Ken then remembered something his father had told him once: "Always buy a rich man a beer; you never know what you will get in return".

Ken necked the last of his now rather warm Corona and gestured to the barman. "Let me get you another. Two more Coronas *por favor*." For some reason Ken was actually feeling rather excited. The aura of this guy seemed to be rubbing off on him. "I'm Ken, by the way."

"Brad." They shook hands in a very English way.

"What made you think that I was unhappy in my job and what do real business owners feel like?" Ken could not seem to stop himself now, almost forgetting to let go of Brad's hand.

"Hey, I hope I didn't upset you, it's the Australian in me, can't help being blunt, it has got me into a bit of trouble in the past, but it's done far more good for me, so I keep at it."

"No offence taken, you are quite close to the mark, so I'm interested in knowing what gave the game away."

"To be honest that one was a bit of a guess based on the other factors, age, profession, and that faraway look of a man going over a big challenge in his head, which is at odds with most of the stress-free holidaymakers in this place."

"Well you were bang on. I'm 45 years old, with 10 years in my dream job, having achieved all my goals, but completely fed up that I am no longer going anywhere, and not wanting to risk what I have built up. I have no idea what I should do. I thought about starting my own business, but it just seems so risky in this economic climate. So I'd be very interested in knowing what got a serial entrepreneur like you started in business."

"Good question," Brad said, smiling, as if he wanted to ensure Ken knew that he was happy answering. "I was 16 when a friend's dad gave me a book called *Rich Dad, Poor Dad* by Robert Kiyosaki. I was just about to sit my exams with a view to going to university as my parents wanted me to do. From then it would likely have been following in my father's footsteps into an accountancy firm, partnership, retirement and death."

Ken was having a certain sense of déjà vu as Brad described his life.

"That book, I can honestly say, changed the course of my life. Well actually it was one concept in the book that did it for me. Have you got a pen?" Brad grabbed a napkin and Ken found a pen in the breast pocket of his shirt. As he pulled it out he realised that only an accountant would have a pen in his pocket in the middle of summer at Disney World. He smiled to himself and handed it to Brad.

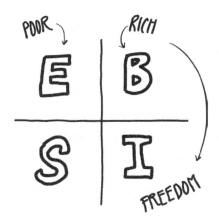

Brad drew a cross and one each of the letters E, S, B and I in each quadrant. "This is what Kiyosaki called the cashflow quadrant and it shows the different ways that you can make money.

"E stands for employee and these guys have to trade time for money. You work you get paid, you don't work you don't get paid. As a result the only way you can earn more money is to work harder or upskill. But there is only so much skill you can have and only so many hours you can work. Does that ring a bell?" he said with that wry smile.

Ken nodded. "That is exactly where I am. I don't want to work any more hours and I am at the top of the tree in my profession, so I am stuck earning what I am earning, and whilst I am comfortable, I know I have more in me. So where do I go from here?"

"Well what most people do is go from the E box to the S box, self-employed." He drew a line straight down. "They are good at the job they do, so they think 'I know, I will go work for myself and become self-employed'. So they give up working for an idiot boss and start working for a complete lunatic: themselves. Because now they are not only doing the job they had before but also all the admin, sales, marketing, finance etc, in most of which they have no experience at all.

"The other thing they have not realised is that they still only have a JOB, trading time for money. OK they are now in total control of their time, but they will always be limited to what they can earn because again they are just trading time for money. The reality is a self-employed person is somebody who would rather work 16 hours a day for themselves than 8 hours for somebody else. Crazy but true."

"I'm with you on that one," Ken chipped in. "I just could not get excited about starting my own accountancy firm, as I would have to go back to doing the work which I have spent 10 years moving away from."

"Bang on," Brad said. "What we need to do is move to the other side of the quadrant. The B is for business owner. Here you run a business that works without you, i.e. you have people working for you, so you are no longer trading your time for money, you are trading other people's time for money. And the more people you employ the more money you can make. In fact if you think of it, there is now no limitation on what you can make, only the limitation you put on yourself."

"Wow you are right. I can see why this was such an eye opener to you at 16; it's blowing my socks off and I'm 30 years older. But how does it get better than that; what is in the I box?"

"Another good question," Brad replied. "The I box is the investor box, and this is where the real wealth in the world is. Here people not only trade other people's time for money, they also trade other people's money for money. It's called leverage. The easiest way to think of this is that when you bought your first house, what did you pay and how much mortgage did you take out?"

Ken gave it some thought. "In 1992 we bought our first house for £60,000 and took out a £40,000 mortgage."

"So you used £20,000 of your own money to buy a £60,000 property, and how much is that house worth now?"

"Well we sold it a couple of years ago for £200,000, having repaid the mortgage in full."

"Excellent, so you had £20,000 and after 20 years this became £200,000 and you borrowed £40,000 from the bank to achieve this, i.e. you leveraged the money you had with the bank to make £140,000, a 700% return on investment. That is leverage, and when you do this on a regular basis, with property and/or businesses, you are able to make money from nothing while not being dependent on the hours you work."

Ken gazed at the numbers Brad had written on the napkin, slightly embarrassed. Here he was, a successful accountant, who knew numbers inside out, yet this was something he was having difficulty accepting. He knew that he had made money on his house, and he remembered his mother saying that there is nothing safer for your money than in the property you lived in, but he had not realised that his borrowing to buy his first property was a good thing. His mother also said, "Never a borrower or a lender be" and "It's best to pay off the mortgage as soon as you can". Yet he could now see that if he had invested £20,000 every five years and bought a house with a mortgage on each he would be far wealthier than he was now.

"Darn!!" Ken exclaimed. "How did I never work this out myself? Here I am, 45, worried about being in the E box and should I move to the S box, when what I should be thinking is how do I move into the B and I boxes."

"You got it Ken," Brad said, with his big infectious smile.

"This is the lesson I learnt when I was 16 and it meant that I started young and in 10 years I was financially free and I retired from working for the first time. The reality though is that retirement is a state of mind and if you spell it 'really – tired', it states most people's view of it, but at 26 I was far from tired, so I just got back on the rollercoaster and have been enjoying the ride ever since."

"But I'm 45, Brad. If I was in my 20s I could do this, but at my age surely it's too late." Ken was starting to doubt himself, thinking of all the reasons it would not work for him.

"Hey buddy, get your fat BUT out of the way. It took me 10 years, and on the basis that you are going to live at least 10 more years, you can do it as quick, if not quicker. After all, you have far more knowledge than I did when I was 16."

"You're right Brad. If I could achieve half of what you have by the time I am 60, then I will be a happy chappy."

Brad laughed at Ken's English. "There you go, now you are thinking BIG. Keep aiming for the stars, Ken, and if you hit the moon you will be doing fine. Look, buddy, I have to go. I said I would meet the kids at 4 and it's a hell of a walk to the water park. "

"Sure thing Brad, look thanks so much for your time today. This has made such an impact on me that my head is now spinning in a completely different way," Ken answered.

"You are going to have to get used to that. If you take the next step you are going to start on the biggest rollercoaster of your life, so you'd better be prepared for one hell of a ride. Just remember you've got to have a really big reason why you want a business and never lose sight of that even in the toughest of situations, because it will be the only thing that can get you through the dips. Oh and one final thing, just remember to enjoy the ride when things are good and learn the lessons when they are not. Thanks for the beer. Here's my card. If you ever visit Vegas I'll return the favour and keep me posted of your progress."

They shook hands, again in a very English way, and Brad strode out of the bar, while Ken clutched the napkin in his hand. He thought to himself, 'by this time next year I am going to be running my own business', and with that the weight that had been on his mind for the first part of the holiday lifted. He almost floated out of the bar to his family and they had a fantastic end to their stay in Florida.

Lesson 2
Life is a mirror

Your life is always a reflection of you, whether you like it or not. Your actions and decisions have brought you to this point in time, whether you dropped out of school with no qualifications, or went to university and came out with a PhD, and whether you got a job and climbed the corporate ladder, or started buying and selling fruit and vegetables at the market.

> *"If you always do what you've always done,*
> *you'll always get what you've always got."*
> Henry Ford (1863–1947)

You chose your route and where you are now is the result. Now you may be happy or sad with this depending on your outlook of where you currently are, but the key thing to remember is that because this is always true, where you will be in the future will be down to the decisions and actions you choose to take from this point forward.

For many, starting a business is the change that they want to give them a better life, be it as a young lad, like Brad, or a more mature individual such as Ken.

Over 500,000 business are started in the UK every year (according to Companies House) and the amazing thing is that there is no qualification or past experience needed to start one, so anybody can do so. It has to be the most inclusive way to achieving a better life.

However, if you are going on this journey, you have to understand that the path from which you enter the business will very much reflect what sort of business you will build.

In his international bestseller, *The E-Myth (Revisited)*, Michael Gerber carried out research to find out why most businesses fail and what to do about it. He found that there were three types of people who start businesses.

The first is the entrepreneur who, like Brad, has no real background in the businesses they get involved with; they just love business. True entrepreneurs usually start quite young; think of Alan Sugar dropping out of school to work on a market stand or Richard Branson starting to sell records from his student flat. These are the people most in business aspire to be like, but the true fact is that less than 5% of businesses are actually started by these people. This fact gave Gerber the inspiration for his title, *The Entrepreneurial (E) Myth*.

You can tell an entrepreneur's business because it is very fast moving. Entrepreneurs like to take risks and see failure as just a stepping stone to success.

Entrepreneurs do not get stuck working in their businesses. Whilst they will always get their hands dirty, especially in the early days, they very quickly hire others to do the work, so that they can focus on building the business.

The second group are managers. Just like Ken, these are people who have worked hard in their jobs and risen through the ranks only to find they no longer enjoy their role, so they leave and normally buy a business or franchise that is already up and running, which they can take over. These people are more common than entrepreneurs, but still only account for 15% of businesses.

Managers like systems and processes and their businesses will reflect this. They go for steady growth, not taking too big a risk. Often they get to a size which they are comfortable at managing and do not push onto the bigger and better things that the entrepreneur would go after.

The third group are the ones that start up most businesses and Gerber calls these the technicians. That is, they are run by people who are trained in the field in which the business operates. A plumber runs a plumbing business, an accountant runs an accountancy business, a dentist a dental practice, and so on. This group accounts for 80% of business start-ups and although this book is based on Ken 'the manager', everything else would apply to the technician and entrepreneur as well.

The technician's business is often the most chaotic. Assuming that it has grown beyond just one self-employed person, because the technician is the master of the job they find it very hard to let go and let other people do the work. They therefore become very busy working IN their business and not working ON it.

Working more hours than any of their staff, fixing all the problems that their staff make, these businesses are the ones that are most likely to fail according to Gerber, and even if they last they are virtually just a glorified JOB for the owner, with less holiday and security than if they worked for somebody else.

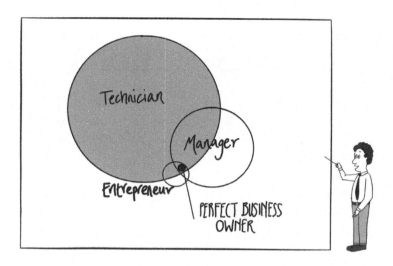

So while there is no entry exam to run a business, you have to under-stand which business owner type you are, and be careful not to allow the business to become a reflection of your current skills. You can do this by ensuring that you take the best of each type, and learn how to become a perfect business owner.

BIG Actions

1. If you are a true entrepreneur, learn from those that have been before you and get help to avoid making too many costly mistakes.

2. Managers need to be pushed to the next level. In your own business you have no boss telling you what to do so you have to keep setting new goals.

3. Technicians need to spend as much time learning how to run a business as they did learning their trade and then train other people to do the work they do.

The BIG Question

On the flight back from the USA, all Ken could think about was starting a business. He had now definitely ruled out starting an accountancy practice. There would be no way he could trust himself not to get sucked into doing the work, but what should he do?

He enjoyed coming up with ideas with his wife and kids, and for the first time in years he was actually feeling excited about life again. He was realising more and more how fed up he had been in his job, and even though the fear of leaving behind the security was there, the enthusiasm of a new venture far outweighed this and it was clearly rubbing off on the family.

He suddenly remembered Brad's comment about starting on the rollercoaster and his feeling was most definitely like that of queuing up for the ride. He was just wishing he could get to the front of the queue a lot quicker.

A month had passed since the holiday. The kids were back at school, he was back in the routine of work, but life was most definitely not the same. Every day he would take a different route to work, looking at the shops and businesses to give him ideas of the business he could start. He looked at businesses for sale online and in the papers, and had even arranged a meeting with a business broker. However, the more he looked, the more confused he got.

What is it that I really want to do? he asked himself, as he reached into his desk drawer and took out a pad. Right, I am going to write a list of the things I want my business to be.

- A local shop front

- Does good for the community

- Not too skills based so I can help out and employing people is easy

- Has repeat business so I can have clients for life

- A business that I can add on products and services, so I won't get bored or have all my 'eggs' in one basket

Over the next few days the list grew and grew, and as a result Ken felt better and better. He then set about ranking the list in order of importance, and when it became full of scribbling he put it into a spreadsheet. As he did this Ken smiled to himself; only an accountant would break down buying a business into a spreadsheet.

Ken happily distracted himself with his lists and research for the next few weeks. However, the more thought he put into it, the more confused he started to become. There were now so many choices he did not know which way to go.

It had always been a tradition for Ken on Friday evenings to leave work a bit early, and stop off at the pub on the way home to meet up with his friends for an end of week chat and pint.

Since returning from holiday, Ken had not made it to the pub, because he had gone straight home to carry out his research. But this Friday he was fed up with his lack of progress so thought he would go to the pub instead. When he arrived he was warmly welcomed by the slightly boisterous middle-aged group at the bar.

"Hey Ken," Ian, the heavily-set guy in painter and decorator overalls, called out. "Where the hell have you been over the last few weeks? We thought you had liked it so much in Florida that you stayed."

Ken smiled. It was good to be with people who cared about him, and after a few kisses, hugs, handshakes, and his first pint of bitter, all present were up to speed with his holiday and he with their lives over the last few months.

However, Ken held something back. Not once did he mention his decision to start his own business or his meeting with Brad, and especially not his list of what his business would be like. On the way home from the pub, Ken reflected on this decision. These were his best friends; they had grown up together and been through a lot of ups and downs together, yet he was scared of telling them. Why was this?

Over the next few weeks Ken came away from the pub with exactly the same feeling. The time never seemed right to talk about it.

That evening Ken mentioned this to his wife Jane, who he had constantly kept in the picture about what he wanted to do since the meeting with Brad in Florida. Jane was a very strong and inde-pendent woman. Not only did she do most of the looking after the kids, but she was also the trustee of a local charity that helped disabled people go to sea to sail on amazing tall ships.

"Well it's obvious why you won't tell them," she said whilst taking the dinner out of the oven. Jane was one of the most astute people Ken knew and he often wondered why he did not ask her advice more frequently. "You are scared that they will say you are an idiot for jacking in the best job of any of them, giving up the security of a pension, healthcare, holidays, nice car, office and everything else you have worked 20 plus years for, on the whim of a man you met at Disney World."

Ken was left a little gobsmacked, but Jane continued.

"And they would be right. But they have not seen you over the last couple of years getting more and more miserable, and if there is one thing that I have learnt working with the charity, life is not about where you are now, it is what you can achieve. I believe in you and so do the kids, and if they are truly your best friends then they will believe in you too. They are only worried for you, so be appreciative that they care enough, but don't let their way of thinking hold you back. So you have got to stop procrastinating and get on and tell them about it. Now eat your dinner!"

Ken knew Jane was right. She was most of the time, so why would this be any different? But it was more than that. This was the first time that he really believed that she was behind him with this decision, and he knew that with her support nothing could stop him.

At the next Friday gathering, Ken decided to partially follow his wife's direction. He was going to sound each one of his friends out on what they thought about starting their own businesses, but without admitting to them that this was what he wanted to do. He thought he would start with Ian, the one who was already working for himself.

Ian had been a painter and decorator since he left school. He had worked first for a large firm, until he was made redundant during the start of the last recession. Since then his business had grown to employing a dozen or so guys, but over the last few years he had downsized to be just him and a couple of self-employed helpers.

He took Ian to one side whilst talking football, and then managed to turn the conversation around to his business. "If you could have your time again Ian, would you do it again?"

Ian looked thoughtful, took a big gulp of lager, then burped. "'Scuse me. No way. I'd never go back to being employed by somebody else for sure. I love the freedom that working on my own gives me, but I would also never go back to employing anybody. They are just a pain in the neck. First off you can't get good ones, then when you think you have they never work as hard as you and when it's quiet they want to be paid, so I ended up doing my job and their job. Then add on trying to run the business as well, I was working seven days a week and the extra money I made was just not worth it. I think I have the balance right now. I know that I will never be rich, but I have a good life and that suits me fine."

Ken could see that Ian had almost made it to the right hand side of the cashflow quadrant that Brad talked about, moving from E to S on redundancy, and then attempting to move to quadrant B. But he had to move back down to S when this proved too much.

So Ian had accepted to himself that he was only ever going to be trading time for money. However, Ken knew that Ian was not daft, and that actually, because of his skills, he was also working in the I quadrant, as every now and then he would buy a rundown house, do it up and rent it out. This was going to be Ian's pension fund when the physical toll of painting and decorating meant he had to hang up his brush.

Ken's next target was Richard, the school teacher. He had never known what he wanted to do as a kid, and Ken was quite jealous that when he was studying at university, Richard was off travelling the world, going from one part-time job to another. He asked him the same question: "If you could have your time over again, would you do the same?"

"Without doubt," Richard said. "I am so glad I got my travelling in when I was young enough to do it and enjoy it, and now I love this job. Giving back and educating others is one of the best feelings you can have. I know it is not that well paid, but I have good holidays so I can continue my love of travel and I also know that I will have a good pension when I retire. I am also very proud that I am making a difference in people's lives every day."

Ken could see that his initial thought, that you had to be on the right side of the quadrant to be successful, was not quite as clear cut as it first seemed.

Richard was clearly in the E box and happy, with his future financial freedom taken care of with a government pension. OK he would have to work until he was 65, but with as many holidays as he got he could see the attraction.

Of the group, Colin was probably the most similar to Ken; he was a partner in a reasonable sized law firm. Having studied as hard as Ken in the early days, Colin stayed with his first firm and worked his way up the ranks until he was able to buy in as one of six partners.

With the same question being asked, Ken was getting to enjoy finding out more about his friends' views on life. Colin's response was the most surprising of the group.

"Frankly NO!! Over the years I have worked to become a specialist in what I do, and frankly I am bloody good at it. People pay me good money for my help and I return that investment with the best advice they will get this side of a top firm in London. I have all the trappings that come with success and I have invested all the excess money I have made into stocks, shares, gold, and pensions, but now there is nowhere for me to go.

"None of the partners are actually driving the firm forward. We say we are going to change but none of us actually do anything about it, and if we do not bring in the fees the firm ceases to be. I had the chance to break away with one of the partners five years ago. He was a bit younger than me and now runs a firm that has grown bigger than ours, but I was too fearful of making the move. So I guess I will see out my final few years being the best I can be and we will either be bought out internally or externally when the remaining partners come to an age they want to exit."

Ken could feel Colin's pain, as it was so close to his own, and relating it back to the cashflow quadrant, he could see that there was actually a bigger S under the self-employed S. This was the 'Specialist', somebody who was so good at what they did that they could charge a very high hourly rate and earn enough money to have a great life and invest for their future.

Ken finally moved on to Julie, who was a sales manager for a local electrical company. Julie was a few years younger than the rest of the group and was in fact Colin's sister. She had always tagged along with the boys when they were younger and was always treated as one of the gang.

"No idea," she said when asked the same question. "I can't change it so why bother even thinking about it. All I know is that I want to be where my boss is. He has the best life of anybody I know. He comes into the office a few hours per week to keep us all informed on what is going on and gives us a kick up the backside, and then he lets us get on with it. I know he has other business ventures around the place, in fact he just bought a big one last month and he is now selling off the bits he does not need. I think he does it for the fun of it now, because there is no way he does it for the money; you want to see his house."

Julie's boss was clearly in the B and I quadrants. This was the life that Ken was after. He drove home that night, deep in reflection. He had never thought of his friends in this way before; in fact he still saw them as kids playing football in the park, but of course they had grown up and they were all clearly in their own sector of the cashflow quadrant. He was sure they were all doing OK, in their own way, but he was not and he was now more determined than ever to become a proper businessman.

Lesson 3
Stop procrastinating

We all have to make difficult decisions, even ones where we have no idea of the outcome. Each one of Ken's friends had made decisions in the past and had no idea that they would lead them to where they were now.

The danger is when there are no immediate consequences of not making a decision or taking action, we tend to procrastinate and avoid doing what we should do.

"I used to procrastinate; now I just think about it."

Procrastination is the killer of dreams. It is the practice of carrying out less important, short-term gratification tasks in preference to more important, long-term benefit ones.

For Ken, he was actually becoming troubled with too many choices about what he could do, and as there was no clear right choice, he could not make the important decision. He found himself becoming busy doing easy stuff such as making lists and thus avoiding having to make a decision.

So how does procrastination start and what can we do to avoid or overcome it?

Well in a very simplistic way, the brain is said to have two sides, left and right. The left is our logical and analytical side while the right is the emotional and creative side. An easy way to remember this is that the left brain also controls the right side of the body and the right brain the left side of the body. Therefore emotional decisions are often said to be decisions of the heart, which of course is on the left side of the body and controlled by the right side of the brain.

However, there are times when we get a blockage in our thinking on one side or other of the brain. A logical blockage is often because of too many facts, choices or no one answer. An emotional blockage comes from being unsure how the decision will make us or other people feel.

Ken's blockage was coming from the choices and decisions he had in front of him. Being an accountant he was likely to be more logically driven and liked to solve problems, but this problem had no actual solution so he was left in a loop.

He may also be experiencing an emotional blockage, because he was unsure how his wife or friends would feel about his decision.

The important thing to remember in these cases is that whichever side the blockage is the only way to overcome it is by engaging the other side of the brain.

So when solving a logical challenge bring in your emotions and when facing an emotional challenge, bring in some logic.

Ken's approach to overcoming his emotional procrastination was to make a logical list of what he wanted and to ask his friends what they had learnt on their journeys. To overcome his logical blockage however, his wife's emotional support was not quite enough. He was about to find out that if you procrastinate for too long your decision is often taken out of your hands.

BIG Actions

1. Spot your own way of procrastinating. Ask someone close to you to call you on it when they see it in you. Check in with yourself regularly and ask yourself if what you are doing is moving you to your goals.

2. When you have an emotional challenge, write down what a good outcome should look like, make a list of pros and cons of the options available to you and then go with the most logical.

3. When you have a logical challenge, tap into your feelings and emotions; ask those close to you what options they can see that you have missed. Trust your gut instinct.

The BIG Push

I t was the week after he had asked all of his friends the key question, and since then Ken had been visualising his ideal business every day. He still did not know what it would be selling, but the way he would run it was getting clearer.

Ken walked into the bar that Friday evening, thinking of another question to ask his friends so he could glean some more information, but he was stopped in his tracks when Julie looked him straight in the eye and said, "Come on, out with it."

"What?" he replied.

"Don't give me that. You've been acting very strange over the last few months, and last week we all felt that we were being interrogated. You're up to something. You know you can trust us, now tell us what it is."

"OK guys, you know me too well," he sighed but was relieved that he no longer had to play games with them, but also aware that there was no going back once he had told them. "You promise that this does not go outside of this group?" They all nodded and muttered yeps and yeses. "I want to quit my job and start my own business." The words came out forcefully, without hesitation, and Ken could feel that now he had verbalised his goal there was something different going on in his head.

He looked at each of them in turn. For a split second they did not seem to get what he had said, and then they all replied at once, so he had trouble in deciphering what was being said.

Ian, Colin and Richard were shaking their heads, while Julie was beaming like a Cheshire cat.

"You're mad, why would you give up such a great job?", said Colin.

"What sort of business are you going to start? There is no way you could replicate the one you are in, so what else are you qualified to do?", chipped in Ian.

"You're not thinking of setting up an accountancy business are you!", Richard said in such a way that made Ken feel like he had just made the worse decision of his life.

Julie could see that Ken's positive demeanour was starting to ebb away. "Hey guys, let's not judge his decision until he has told us more. Go on, Ken, tell us why you want to change."

Ken then spent the next 30 minutes informing his friends of how bored he was with his job, his meeting with Brad and his discussion with Jane. "... And so all I need now is a business idea," he concluded.

Richard was the first to speak. "I still don't see why you would give up what you have to start something fresh. There is no security with your own business and if you don't make it you won't be able to go back to where you are now."

"Richard is right," Colin interjected. "Employing people is a pain in the neck. I could see you being a self-employed accountant, but how is that going to give you more than what you already have? I know I could not do it; even if the partnership changed for the worse, I would need that support structure around me."

Ken was by now wishing that he had not said anything. All his friends seemed against the idea and the doubts that he thought he had got rid of were all coming back. It felt like he had just sat in the front seat of the rollercoaster and everybody else had walked away, muttering that the ride was just far too dangerous.

Then Julie piped up. "Hey guys, I think you are being a little unfair. I think it's great news, totally bonkers in some respects, but totally awesome in others. I've seen my boss make millions through his businesses and I know you are far smarter than he is, Ken, so if he can do it, so can you." She leant over and gave him a big hug. Well at least now there was one other person sitting by his side on the rollercoaster.

Two weeks passed and the topic of a business did not really come up again with his friends. He kept on talking about it with his wife, but he did not want the negative vibes that he thought his friends would give him.

Then disaster struck!

It was Wednesday evening. Ken was wrapping up for the day when his boss David knocked politely on his door and asked if he had a few minutes before he left. They both sat on the leather suite that he had in his room for the more informal meetings.

"Do you want the good news or the bad news?" David said gravely. "Good news I suppose," Ken said, wanting to delay the bad news as he felt it was going to be pretty bad. He had never had a conversation like this with David all the time he had been in the role.

"Well, the good news is our company has been sold to the French for a rather large sum of money, so your share options are going to be worth cashing in."

This was good news. Ken had known that there had been talks in the past, but the offers were never good enough to sell, so this should mean that more money was on the cards. "That's great, and the bad news?"

"They want to wrap the whole deal up in 3–6 months and are moving the entire finance department to France, so you have either got to learn French or find another job."

David and Ken had never really got on well and Ken detected just a hint of pleasure when David came out with this. It was as if he was seeing it as an act of revenge for some past misdemeanour.

"Wow, I was not expecting that, what is going to happen to the rest of the operation?" Ken asked. David then went on to inform Ken of the entire plan, and when they finally said their goodbyes, Ken was left with feelings of anger for not being informed of this sooner, and excitement because he could now see an open door to escape through. The rollercoaster was about to leave the platform.

Lesson 4
Drive or be driven

Newton's first law of motion states that "an object remains at rest unless acted upon by an external force". For example a rollercoaster car will not move from the platform unless a force propels it forward. This is a universal law and therefore applies to all things, including us as humans.

Our brains use electric impulses from our neurons to create ideas which are then built on through our senses of sight, sound, feeling, taste and smell, and the energy builds until an action is taken.

Ken was at rest in his job, until a spark of an idea that he was not happy formed in his conscious brain. Then through his actions, additional external forces acted on him: the meeting with the BIG man, and the discussions with his wife and friends. The energy of the original idea was built on and if this energy continued to be built on over time, would have been enough to make Ken take action.

Unfortunately, the outside world never stays still for long, and if you are not providing the force yourself it will provide a force for you that will speed up this process and actually take it out of your hands.

This is so true of people like Ken who have a tendency to procrastinate, as we saw in the previous chapter. They just become pawns in what is going on in their worlds, because they never have enough internal energy to dictate their own path.

Think of it like the difference between being thrown into the rollercoaster car and hurtled off when you are still thinking about going on the ride, as opposed to getting in the car, preparing yourself mentally, being told that the ride is about to go and then starting the ride.

One leads to stress, the other to excitement.

So when you think of it, exactly the same situation can give rise to two completely different emotions.

This is why planning is such an important part of running a business. It gives your brain time to access possible outcomes so that it feels as if it is in control and able to make the first move, rather than being forced to move. However, too much planning and no action will allow external forces to take over and start the ride before you are ready.

Newton also adds that the object will then move at a constant velocity unless acted upon by another force. E.g. the rollercoaster car will slow or speed up when it hits a rise or a dip as the force of gravity interacts with it. This means that you will always have the ability to change the direction in which you are travelling, even if you did not start the ball rolling, and before another force stops you in your tracks.

As we will see Ken is going to have a few internal and external forces acting on him over the coming years.

BIG Actions

1. When you have an idea, work hard to build on it to a point where you take action or dismiss it.

2. Make plans not for the plan itself but for the process that you will go through so you have the confidence to move forward.

3. If the outside world takes over, don't panic. You still have the ability to affect the outcome; just re-plan and take back control.

The BIG Opportunity

Ken's mixed emotions continued for the rest of the week, and although Jane had done her best to talk to him, he wanted to hear what his friends had to say about it.

He got to the pub that Friday a little early and made his way to the bar to order a drink. The guy next to him wished him a good evening and Ken – contrary to his normal shy retiring nature – acknowledged him and asked if he had had a good week.

The conversation was the normal strangers in a pub talk about nothing in particular, until the man asked Ken what he did for a living. For a second Ken was stunned into silence. 'What was he?' he could hear himself think, an accountant, finance director, unemployed or a wannabe business owner?

Ken had already gleaned that this guy was visiting from out of town and was unlikely to bump into Ken again. So he thought he would put on a little act.

"I'm a business investor and I am looking for a suitable business to invest in right now." The words felt really good and his confidence grew even more when the stranger seemed to be impressed.

"Interesting," the stranger replied. "What sort of business are you looking for?"

Ken's confidence suddenly fell away. It was ages since he did his list of what he wanted in a business, and, being put on the spot, he could not remember a single one of them.

"Oh something with growth potential in a marketplace that is of interest. I want to get in and run it rather than being a hands-off investor," he blagged, trying to keep it as vague as possible.

"Well I might be able to help. My uncle has a sign business that he wants to sell. I've been telling him for years to grow it or sell it but he's been happy as it is. Last year though he had a heart attack and the doctor has said he should retire. I know he wants to make sure it goes to a good home as he's had it for 40 years. Give me your details and I'll put you in touch."

They exchanged cards, chatted for a little while longer and said their goodbyes. Ken was left shell-shocked, not really knowing what had happened. Had he really found a business to buy, from a stranger in a pub? A few minutes later Julie and Ian arrived, followed swiftly by Colin and Richard. "You'll never guess what's happened to me this week," Ken said excitedly, as he began to recount the whole story from the sale of the business to the conversation with the stranger, in a way that only a highly detailed person could ever do.

"Wow," said Ian, "there is some strange 'law of attraction' going on here. What are you going to do now?"

"No idea; it's all happened so fast that I'm worried I'll take a quick decision that I'll live to regret."

Julie was the voice of reason. "Well nothing is certain as yet so why not go with the flow, keep us posted and run it by us before you make any decisions."

"Good idea, now I'd better go home and tell Jane what has just happened."

Over the next few weeks the details of the takeover became clearer, and after discussing it with Jane, they both agreed that they did not want to move to France and the business idea was a goer. This decision was backed up when Ken found out that if he chose to take redundancy he would be paid one year's salary and could keep his car. This would mean that he did not have to earn anything from the business for 12 months and with his savings, cashing in his share options and some equity in the house, he felt he could raise another £250,000 to fund the acquisition.

The stranger's uncle got in contact and Ken spent many weeks with financial statements, budgets and cashflows. All of which he was as happy as a 'pig in muck' with. He put the figures into spread-sheets, produced pages of ratios and analysis, all with the purpose of proving to himself that this was a good business opportunity. He researched the marketplace, checked the competition, and did as much due diligence work as he could think of.

The business was called Ray Signs. It was not a big company. It had three members of staff plus the uncle, was based in a rather shabby factory, and had the general feeling of quite a few years of neglect. This all made Ken very happy as he knew he could do something with it and the price he could offer was going to be low, allowing Ken to have money left to put the improvements he wanted in place.

All thoughts of other businesses had left Ken's mind. This was the only one on the cards and rather than find reasons not to buy it, Ken was doing what anybody who has set their heart on something does, and only looking for reasons why he should go ahead.

This included avoiding the questions that his friends posed to him every Friday night. They just seemed to ask him questions that were finding fault in the business, and he got so fed up with them that he purposefully missed more visits than he made over the ensuing weeks.

Eventually the day came when he had to make an offer. The uncle had informed Ken that there was another interested party and that he wanted to move quickly but needed the asking price. Ken had always seen himself as a good negotiator when it came to his current employer's money, but now it was his. When he was emotionally attached to the outcome, he seemed more averse to haggling than he would have been if he was doing it on behalf of his soon to be former employer.

Ken's offer was accepted on the spot, always a good sign that it was too high! Ken kicked himself, but he actually did not care; he was going to be his own boss within a few weeks. All that was left now was to say goodbye to his old work colleagues, clear his desk and get ready for the first day of his new life. The rollercoaster was off and running.

Lesson 5
See the opportunities

There is no such thing as 'LUCK'. Golfer Ben Hogan summed it up best: "The harder I practise the luckier I get." Some would say that both Ken's chance meetings were down to luck, but the reality is that he could have had a beer and a conversation and walked away.

They say that opportunity is all around us, if we just open our eyes and look. Some people call this the 'Law of Attraction'. This has been written about in many ways from Napoleon Hill's *Think and Grow Rich!*, to Rhonda Byrne's *The Secret*.

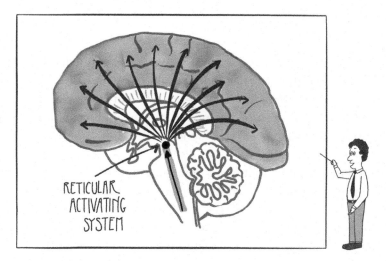

These are both great books, but the concept is actually simpler to comprehend if you think of how the human brain works. There is a part of the brain called the Reticular Activating System (RAS). This is a receptor that decides what information is passed to the rest of the brain to be processed.

Think of it this way. Your five senses are taking in information all the time. You do not stop and start hearing, seeing, tasting, feeling or smelling; they are constantly switched on. If you were conscious of this information all the time your brain would go into overload and you would not know what was important and what was just background noise.

Your RAS acts as a filter, only allowing what it sees as important information to pass through to be processed by the brain. Try this for a little test. Look around the room and count up all the red things you see. Now write that number down. So how many blue things were there? Yes, I do mean blue. I bet you hardly noticed any at all. That is simply because you set your RAS to look for red things and thus ignored all the blue things.

This is also why they say that those who are 'pint half empty' people always see the negative in life, while the 'pint half full' people see the positive. We have to be very careful in life to only programme our RAS with the good things that we want so that it can see the opportunities that will get us there.

So in the context that faced Ken, he set his RAS by focusing on what he wanted, which meant that whenever he came across something that helped him achieve his goal he noticed it and was able to take action. The only downside was that he was so focused on this goal that he had shut out useful information that might have got him a better price, or enabled him to see that the deal was not all that it was cracked up to be.

BIG Actions

1. Start programming your Reticular Activating System (RAS) by setting positive goals and put yourself into situations where opportunities are likely to be. There's no use sitting at home waiting for things to happen.

2. Always look for the opportunity in every situation, no matter how bad things get. If you keep a positive perspective you will see a positive way forward.

3. Be careful about setting too small a goal, because you may programme your RAS to ignore vital information that could stop you achieving more.

The BIG
Ride

As Ken walked into the Ray Signs office on his first day, there was no fanfare, no applause, no welcome banners. He felt more like the new apprentice on his first day rather than an experienced businessman. Ray, the uncle, had agreed to stay on in the business for six months so he could help Ken get to grips with the business. He was there to welcome Ken with a warm handshake that did little to alleviate Ken's nervous tension.

Ray had shown Ken around the place a few times during the purchase and due diligence work, but it had always been out of working hours and so he had not met the team properly. There was Nick in sales, Robert in production and Pam in admin. They all stood in the reception area like a small group of naughty school children, not knowing whether to make eye contact, say something or run and hide.

Ken had thought of a big speech, but it had seemed a little over the top for such a small group. He had therefore agreed with himself that he would give a short explanation of his history and what had brought him to this point, and then ask each of them to do the same.

Nick was in his 50s with the weathered look of a man who had been there, done that, got the t-shirt and used it to clean the floor. It turned out that he had been in sales most of his life, selling for larger businesses until he was made redundant in the last recession, which Ken noted he still seemed to be bitter about seven years later.

Robert was younger, mid to late 30s, with a wife and young daughter. He had been with the company since leaving school on an apprenticeship and had huge respect for Ray.

Pam was in her 60s, and looked like a school teacher with her half-rim spectacles on her nose. She was part time and had worked with Ray most of her life, so she knew exactly how he ticked. Ken could see that she was a key figure in the smooth running of the business.

After the pleasantries, the team went off to work and Ken went into Ray's room to talk further, and begin his learning curve about the day to day running of the business.

Over the next few weeks Ken's learning curve seemed never ending. In his former role he could focus on one area of the business and do that really well. In addition he had staff to delegate work to and a boss to report to. He was beginning to see that owning a business had far more roles and responsibilities, which were all going to fall on his shoulders.

Ken was obviously going to be happy working on the financial aspects of the business. He knew he had a bit of work to do on the accounts system, which was very old and relied on a multitude of spreadsheets to keep track of what was happening. However, when Ray started talking about the sales pipeline, customer relationships, production plans, delivery schedules, wages, appraisals and marketing, Ken started to think that, despite all the years he had been working in a business, he knew so little.

Over the next few weeks, Ken started to get to grips with the basics, and was pleased that Ray had agreed to stay on to help and fill in the gaps as they came across them. The relationship with the team was good and it started to feel like a family; they chatted regularly, helped each other out when needed, and even went out for a drink after work.

Ken had been prepared to put in the effort in the early days, starting early and finishing late and coming in on the weekend to catch up. Jane was happy with this and very supportive, knowing that it was important to get the business up and running and for Ken to find his feet.

Every day was different and the buzz Ken got from this was great. He was feeling so much more alive than in his previous role. He was learning new things, improving every week, and building great relationships with his team, customers and suppliers. He even enjoyed the occasional visit from the bank manager and his accountant. The change from his previous job was amazing; he was certainly starting to enjoy the ride.

The first six months whizzed by, and it came as a real surprise when Ray came in and said it was about time that he stood down and let Ken get on with things on his own. He assured Ken that he would be around, but he had plans for a long holiday and was now ready for his retirement. Ken was going to be flying solo, and would soon realise that it is not as easy on your own as it seems.

Ken had bought a successful business, there were some good clients, the team were very efficient and profits and cash were being made on a weekly basis. With Ray gone, Ken oversaw the production schedules to make sure Robert had the stock to do the work. He liaised with Nick to ensure the new and existing customers were happy and to oversee the preparation of the quotes. Then he worked with Pam to make sure they were invoiced and monies collected.

New work came in fairly regularly from their existing sources, referrals and the odd bit of networking that Nick did. There was generally enough to keep Robert and Pam happy and Ken was pleased that everything was running smoothly.

Before he knew it a year had passed and, being the accountant, Ken got involved with preparing the year end accounts. He had a good relationship with the external accountants, who helped with the tax work.

The bank account was healthy, and Ken was able to take a dividend from the profits which paid for a new car for Jane and the kids had great Christmas presents. He gave the team a pay rise and bonus, and there had even been funds to bring in an apprentice for Robert, as there was more work to do, and a sales assistant for Nick, because he said he was busy and wanted somebody to do more of the paperwork.

Every day was a busy day for Ken; he liked to have an open door policy where his team could pop in and speak to him any time they liked, which did seem to be most days. In part he enjoyed solving their problems and it was good to know what was going on in every area of the business.

Things were so good, in fact, that Ken did not mind that he was still working the longest of everybody, always the first in the office and always the last to leave. He also did not mind working the odd weekend when he fell behind on the accounts, because he was helping the team with their jobs.

He also did not mind the fact that he had not had more than a weekend off in the last 12 months, because he was the one who had to cover for the others when they went on holiday.

The second year went much the same as the first year. Although Ken did manage to get a couple of weeks' holiday, he did have to work twice as hard in the week before and the week after, and he was called at least once a day for matters that the team could not fix on their own.

When Ken came to look at the figures for the second year, they were much the same as the first year. It was enough for him to live on, but the amount he was taking home each month was not much more than he had been getting when he was employed, and he seemed to be working twice as hard.

Although Ken was still enjoying the ride he was starting to wonder if he was being a bit of a busy fool, stuck in his version of 'groundhog day'. The rollercoaster was taking him off on a ride and he most definitely was not in control of it.

Lesson 6
Work ON not IN your business

When you run a business, managing your time is one of the key skills you have to master, because there will always be more things to do that you never have time for. It is very easy to think that you are busy and achieving things when in fact you are, like Ken, actually just a busy fool.

What you have to remember is that in a business there are two types of work: working IN and working ON your business. The difference, whilst subtle, will impact on whether you move your business forward, or stay stuck at the same level forever.

Working IN your business is the day to day work that is required to get things done. Things like quotes, invoicing, making things, and meeting customers. This is work that could and should be done by one of your team.

Working ON your business is your thinking, strategy and planning time. It is your time meeting with your team to help them move forward, not solving their challenges.

Stephen Covey, in his international bestseller, *The Seven Habits of Highly Effective People*, said that habit number three was to put first things first. He showed that effective people know how to distinguish between urgent and important work, as shown in his Time Matrix® below.

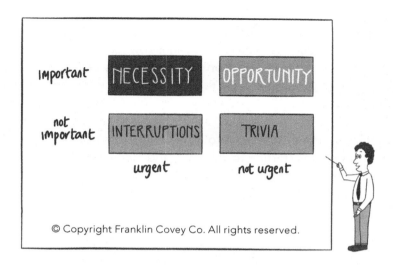

Important tasks are those that will help you achieve your goals. Something becomes urgent when the consequences of not doing it become imminent.

So if you are doing work that is not important and not urgent, you are being distracted and doing trivial work.

Urgent but not important work means you are being interrupted by other people's important and urgent work.

If it is both important to you and urgent then there is a necessity to get this done, often because it was left to the last minute because you were preoccupied with the other two preceding areas.

The last, and most relevant to working ON your business, are the important but not urgent tasks. Those that help you move towards your goals but have no urgency to be done right now. It is this work that Covey says effective people make time to do more of and thus become more successful.

For Ken he was clearly working most of his time in the first three areas, although, as with most business owners I have ever met, there is not a lot of time spent on trivia; it is mainly urgent work which is created by customers, the team or other outside influences such as the bank.

Ken was not making time to work ON the business and as such the business was starting to stagnate, and feel out of his control. As we shall find out, this is not good when times are good, and is disastrous when things take a change for the worse.

BIG Actions

1. Whenever you feel you do not have enough time, start by keeping a daily time audit of the hours you spend each week in each area of your business.

2. Then set the number of hours you should spend in each area in order to move your business forward. Make sure you have enough working ON your business (important but not urgent) time.

3. Book out the working ON activities in your diary and do not compromise these unless you really have to, and if you do you must rebook the time immediately.

The BIG
Dip

Year three went by just as quickly as the first two. Sales continued to grow steadily, but profits stayed the same because a couple more production staff were taken on to meet the demands. There were also the additional sales and marketing costs of the website, advertising and brochures, but Nick was insistent that the big investment would pay off soon.

Ken was spending less time reviewing the finances, partly because Pam was able to do them, partly because he was too busy doing other stuff, but mainly because they were always fairly similar to the previous weeks and months. When he was in his FD role, there were so many aspects of the business to monitor and so many people wanting their numbers that it was a full-time role just keeping up with it. In his business he knew what was going on in every aspect, so why did he need to bother? He now felt that budgets, cashflow forecasts and management figures were for bigger businesses, and as long as there was money in the bank he was happy.

The day it happened was no different to any other day. There was no warning and there was nothing that Ken could have done to avoid it. It started with a phone call from their key client Maddison & Co, a chain of retail shops who were halfway through a shop refurbishment phase, with a contract that was worth £100,000 to Ray Signs over the next 12 months.

This had been Ken's largest order since he had taken over the company, and as such he had made sure he built a very strong relationship with their CEO Joe, who made the call.

"Hi Ken, sorry to bother you this morning, but I felt I had to ring you in person as I have some bad news. Our parent company has gone bust and brought us down with them. We are in a bit of a state here, as you can imagine, but I know this contract was big for you and I wanted you to hear it from me rather than when it goes public in the next hour or so."

Ken was poleaxed. His head was suddenly full of questions he wanted to ask Joe, but deep down he knew it was useless. The only question that mattered was, "Will we get paid for the work we have already done?"

"I can't officially answer that Ken, but between you and me, I think it is doubtful. I am so sorry, but I will let you know if anything changes."

Ken was not on top of his numbers but he knew instantly that while they could survive without this income, it was big enough to have an impact on profits, and set them back over three years on their sales growth. He also knew that he had been allowing them extra terms on their credit, as Joe had become a friend and he had never liked chasing the money. He would have to check but he feared a bad debt would lose them about £20,000 of cash. Needless to say this was going to have a major impact on the business, but this was only the start of the day from hell.

Ken was a large man, just over 6 foot tall and 15 stone, and although now going a little thin on top, he had the remains of some very fine red hair. It is said that red-haired people have fiery temperaments and this was very true for Ken.

In the last three years Ken had always been calm and mild mannered, and apart from hard work, there had been no real stressful moments. The last time he had been put under real stress was with his previous boss. There had been a couple of run-ins and after one occasion Ken was forced to see the Human Resource officer and have a behavioural profile carried out.

This had shown his profile as a cautious, calculating individual with dominant tendencies, which meant that he was like a sleeping dragon, which when awoken could do a lot of damage.

This phone call had clearly upset Ken and although he did not see it, the dragon in him had clearly been awoken. The problem was that the next person through the door was likely to get the first breath of fire, and unfortunately for Ken it was the meek and mild-mannered Pam.

In the three years of working with Ken, Pam had not put a foot wrong. She diligently got on with her work, never complained, was always courteous, punctual and seemingly happy. Ken knew that she was the key to the smooth running of the business from day one and this had proved to be the case. She knew most of the customers by their first names, knew the bookkeeping and filing system inside out, and if he needed anything, Ken knew that she would either know the answer or know who to ask to find out.

But during this time Ken had not felt that he had built any form of relationship with Pam. She was a lot older and thus they had little in common outside of work. He felt that she was a plodder. Jobs that Ken felt should have been done in 10 minutes took an hour, and when Ken wanted something that minute, he would find that she wanted to finish what she was doing before starting his request. And she was a tea-oholic. It seemed like every 15 minutes she was popping her head around the corner and asking if he would like a "nice cuppa tea".

Ken had been prepared to put up with these foibles, because of her knowledge, and the fact that at 63 it would not be long before she would decide to wind down, and Ken could then look at bringing in somebody slightly more dynamic in a few years' time.

That morning, tea was obviously the last thing on Ken's mind and the sight of Pam's face at the door offering the beverage made him snap. After the event, Ken could remember little of what he said, save for a few adjectives such as 'stupid, idiotic, old and brainless'. The result, though, would remain in Ken's memory for a long time. The sight of a 63-year-old lady in tears is not a nice one. However the worst was yet to come.

Nick had the banter of a great salesperson, and when in front of the right people he was one of the best. He had won a few accounts over the last three years, but Ken was never quite sure what he filled his time with. Whenever he confronted Nick on this, he always had a great reason: working on the website, visiting important customers, following up on leads. They had even taken on a sales administrator so that Nick could focus more on being in front of people; it was just that it never seemed to result in enough sales.

Robert was a grafter for sure. If a job needed doing he would be there to do it. He was also a perfectionist, never letting a sign out of the factory unless it was 'good enough for the Queen', but delegation was not his strong point, and the three team members they had recruited to take on some of the basic work seemed to drink more tea than Pam.

Nick and Robert had heard the commotion and came in to see what was going on. After calming Pam down, Nick and Robert came into Ken's office, rather fired up themselves.

"What the hell was all that about?" Nick gesticulated towards Pam.

"You cannot treat her like that," Robert added.

Ken had not calmed down since shouting at Pam. In fact he had used the time to look at the aged debtor account and production schedule, only to find out that they were owed closer to £30,000 and had work in progress of £20,000.

"Maddison & Co has just gone bust. Yes, that is right, your bloody client has taken us for nearly £50,000 and without their income next year we are back to where we were three years ago." Ken stared at Nick with the veins on his head pumping like a racehorse in the Grand National. "And as for you, Rob, if you had got that damned work out on time, and Pam had not been so soft on chasing them, we would not be in this mess at all. So don't you come in here telling me what I can and can't say, it's my business and I'll do exactly what I want. Now get back to work, take Pam with you and close the door on your way out."

Ken had had bad days at the office in his previous job. Days when nothing seemed to go right, where his plans were sabotaged by others, where he had made mistakes that could have been costly, where other people had left him with a big problem to solve, and where he had to bust a gut to make amends. Some of these days had turned into weeks and weeks into months. But this was different.

This felt 100 times worse. In his previous job he could always keep a separation between himself and his job. He had a team who were there to help him fix things, people he could order to do work for him, fellow directors who were in the same boat who would join forces to overcome the challenges face on, and a boss who would be in the firing line as much as he would if they could not fix the issue. In addition, it was never his business, not his money on the line and in the worst case scenario, if he lost his job, he knew he could go and get another.

What Ken was feeling was a real sense of failure and loneliness. While he had not started the business, he had taken over responsibility for it, and grown to love it like his own. His baby was now being attacked and he was determined to do what he could to protect it; it was just that he had made the situation worse in doing so.

His team hated him, he had lost their largest customer, and there was nobody around to help him sort out the mess. His rollercoaster had hit its first big downer.

Lesson 7
Be above the line

Jack Canfield, author of *The Success Principles*, has a little formula:

Event + Response = Outcome

Canfield goes on to explain that if you don't like the outcome you are experiencing, then don't go blaming the event, as rarely do you have any influence over it. Instead look at your response to the event and change that to give you a different outcome.

There are two types of people in the world, those who live their lives above the line and those who live below. Above the line people take responsibility for their actions, allow themselves to be held accountable and take full ownership of their lives. Below the line people blame others, make excuses or just live in complete denial.

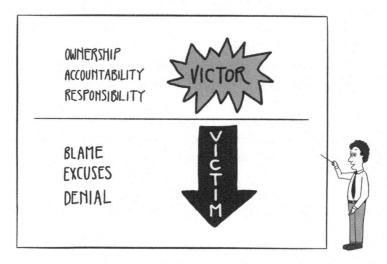

We all know the below the line people. They are the whingers and moaners in life. Spending more than a few minutes with these people can suck the life out of anybody. One of the biggest issues is that they do not realise that they are that way, especially if they have managed to convince others to behave in a similar way.

Ken could do nothing about the loss of the client. He had a choice of being a victim and going below the line, going into blame, excuses and denial, or being a victor, showing above the line behaviour and doing something about it.

Negative responses rarely work, but they are quicker and easier to apply, because they are hardwired into us as human beings. All animals have a fight or flight mechanism which is there to protect them from harm, and under pressure it will be the first line of defence. This is clearly what happened to Ken. Blaming the team for an event out of their control seemed daft in the cold light of day, but in the heat of the moment it made total sense.

What was needed was a different response. As humans we have a higher cognitive thought process than animals, which allows us to solve problems. So where a deer will run from a predator or a cobra will attack it, humans are able to rationalise the problem and come up with alternatives that, while slower and sometimes harder to implement, have a far better long-term outcome.

The challenge is the longer we stay below the line, the harder it is to get back above the line, especially as we will attract other below the line people who will reinforce our negative beliefs.

Ken needs to change his response quickly from one of below the line to being above the line, but this is not as easy as it sounds.

BIG Actions

1. When things go bad focus on the outcome you want and your next step, rather than the event/s over which you have no control.

2. Always take responsibility for every situation. This is your business and as such the buck stops with you. Even if your team let you down, you hired them so it is still down to you.

3. Never make decisions or give feedback to your team in the heat of the moment: you will be in fight or flight mode and may not be thinking rationally.

The BIG Pull

Ken went home that evening totally depressed. His pride had prevented him from apologising to Pam, and he did not want to confront Robert or Nick, so he had kept himself to himself in his area of comfort, playing with the numbers. He had redone budgets and cashflows to see what the effect of the loss of the client would be.

Jane knew something was up the minute he entered the house. Ken came home most evenings late and tired but full of enthusiasm. Today he was early, and hardly said a word. Once the kids were in bed she poured a couple of glasses of wine and sat down next to Ken. "What's the matter love?" she asked in her most comforting and caring voice.

"It's all gone wrong!" Ken would not look at her and was staring at the wall with a vacant look about him.

"What could possibly have happened today that's made you feel this way so quickly?" Jane was totally surprised by his statement.

Ken then slowly recounted the events of the day, culminating in the fact that the cashflow showed that if they could not replace the £30,000 bad debt and at least some of the lost income they had two months before, they would run out of cash very soon.

"I feel like quitting," Ken sighed. "Perhaps I am not cut out for this business lark. I was totally lost today when I got the news and I reacted so badly to the others. How am I going to turn this around? I feel like I have gambled everything on black and it has come in red. I should have realised that I am just an employee and will always be one. Business is for entrepreneurs who are happy taking risks, and have investors that back them up and bail them out when they need help."

Jane was a wise woman and knew that giving advice to Ken was not the solution he needed right now. She could come up with a few ideas, but his analytical mind would find reasons why none of them would work. She therefore did the best thing she could do: give him support, love and understanding that whatever happened going forward, as long as they were together they would make it work.

Ken went to bed that night feeling no better, but thankfully no worse. He was sure that there was an answer somewhere; he was just not going to find it that night.

The following week went past in a blur. He had managed to speak to Pam the next day and smooth over the waters enough for her to agree to come back to work. Nick and Robert had listened to what he had to say about the loss of the business, and whilst they under-stood the implications, he was disappointed but not surprised that neither of them had any real answers about what they should do to overcome the challenge.

On the Tuesday he managed to meet with his accountant who helped him review his costs and finalise the budget to take to the bank on Thursday. The result of that meeting was actually quite positive. Because Ken had always kept the bank manager updated with management figures he was amenable to increasing the overdraft and providing a loan to cover the loss of the bad debt, which would keep the company trading for a few months.

Although this was the last thing that Ken and Jane wanted to do, especially as it meant taking out additional security on their house, with the time they had the only other option would have been to call in an insolvency firm to put the company into administration.

By Friday the immediate panic of survival had abated. Ken had bought himself some time, but time to do what? Nobody he had spoken to that week had come up with any ideas on replacing the lost income and if he could not do this then the game would be over anyway. The more Ken thought about it, the more desolate he felt. Why was he in business if this is what it did to you? Three years of hard work and for what? The business gave him an income of not much more than he had when he was working but with longer hours, less holiday and, as he had just found out, far less job security.

Ken knew he had one last place to get some good advice: his friends at the pub. Although he had not been a regular over the last few years, he had been once or twice a month and enjoyed telling them about his successes with the business, and they always seemed to enjoy listening. Ken was a little apprehensive because he had enjoyed being the success story of the group over the last few years, and the events of this week would put all that into question. However, what are friends for, if not to give you some support in your darkest hours, or so he thought!

As Ken stood by the bar ordering the first round of drinks, Ian chipped in with, "Wow, you look like you have found a penny and lost a pound".

"It's worse than that," Ken sighed. "Let's get the beers in and I'll bring you all up to speed."

After Ken had recounted the story of the week to his friends, he was slightly taken aback by their lack of real understanding of the situation. Colin, the solicitor, said he should cut back his costs, downsize and ride it out. Richard, the teacher, suggested he call it a day and get a 'proper job'. Ian, the painter, came up with the "… told you that employing people was a pain" comment and that he should sack them all and just run the business on his own. Only Julie, the sales rep, had a positive idea, saying he could borrow some more money and trade his way out.

He had entered the pub that evening hoping that his friends would give him the solution to his problem. He left more confused than before he arrived, with conflicting ideas and still no way forward that he felt comfortable with. Perhaps closing the business before things got worse might actually be the best option after all.

That weekend Ken was feeling very depressed, so much so that he did not go to the office, as he knew that it would just make him feel worse. Instead he thought he would spend some time with the kids. Their carefree approach to life would be a good distraction from his worries and concerns about the business.

Whilst in the park pushing them on the swings, Ken's mind drifted to thoughts about giving up on the business, walking away from his investment and leaving the team, suppliers and customers to the hands of the insolvency people, whom the bank would appoint when they realised that he could not repay his loans.

He had no real feeling for the suppliers; they were generally big corporates who would barely flinch at his demise. His customers would go elsewhere. As for the team, Pam would retire, Robert could go and work for any sign company in the area, and he had no real feelings for Nick, and as a salesman, Nick would sell himself into a new role easily. The others had only been with them a year or two and he was sure that they could go and find other jobs quite quickly.

As for Ken, well he was still a qualified accountant and he could still go back and get a good job in industry or even go back into an accountancy practice. Ken was starting to feel like he had when he was fed up with his job and before he decided to buy the business three years ago.

But if he went back to having a job, surely he would just be going back to being unhappy again. This realisation seemed to wake him up! This WAS his dream and to do anything but running a business would be to give up on that dream. Nobody was going to give him a solution to his problem; he was the problem. This business would succeed or fail on his decisions and he had to stop with the self-pity and focus on what he wanted to achieve.

His mind suddenly went back to his first conversation with Brad in the bar in Disney and the words he spoke as they were leaving. "Just remember you've got to have a really big reason WHY you want a business and never lose sight of that even in the toughest of situations. It will be the only thing that can get you through the dips."

Ken had not really understood the comment at the time, but what he did realise was that he was now in a tough situation and he needed to pull himself out. Over the last three years he had lost sight of his WHY. He had got so engrossed with the day to day of the business he had forgotten the reasons he started it in the first place. The negativity of losing that big client was pulling him down and he was finding it hard to fight back.

The rollercoaster had got to the bottom of the track and would need a strong pull to get to the top again.

Lesson 8
Watch what pulls you

Wikipedia gives this definition of gravity:

> "Gravity or gravitation is a natural phenomenon by which all things with mass are brought toward (or gravitate toward) one another, including planets, stars and galaxies. Since energy and mass are equivalent, all forms of energy, including light, also cause gravitation and are under the influence of it.

> "On earth, gravity gives weight to physical objects and causes the ocean tides. The gravitational attraction of the original gaseous matter present in the universe caused it to begin coalescing, forming stars — and the stars to group together into galaxies — so gravity is responsible for many of the large scale structures in the universe. Gravity has an infinite range, although its effects become increasingly weaker on farther objects."

Gravity is most accurately described by the general theory of relativity (proposed by Albert Einstein in 1915) which describes gravity not as a force, but as a consequence of the curvature of space–time caused by the uneven distribution of mass/energy. The most extreme example of this curvature of space–time is a black hole, from which nothing can escape once past its event horizon, not even light.

Gravity is well approximated by Newton's law of universal gravitation, which postulates that gravity causes a force where two bodies of mass are directly drawn (or 'attracted') to each other according to a mathematical relationship, where the attractive force is directly proportional to the product of their masses and inversely proportional to the square of the distance between them.

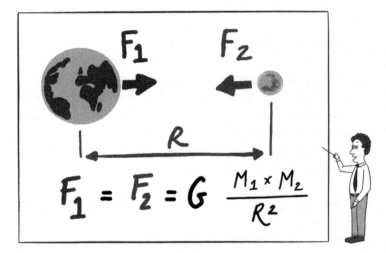

So if you want the gravitational force between the two objects to increase then you have to either close the gap or increase the mass of one or both of the objects.

So how is any of this relevant to us and Ken? Well in Ken's case, the 'gravitational' force between him and his goal of having a business that worked without him had reduced, because of the following two factors:

The first is that the distance between him and his goal had grown. He had not given it a second thought in three years, being more caught up in the day to day activity of the business.

Secondly, the mass of the problems he was facing was now bigger than his goal, so the 'black hole' of his problems was having a bigger gravitational pull than the 'sun' of his original goal of having a commercial, profitable business that worked without him.

By refocusing on what he wanted rather than on what he did not want, Ken would be able to break out of a downward spiral of negative gravity and get himself back on course to his BIG goal.

BIG Actions

1. Always be adding mass to your goals, review them constantly, and build on them so they keep pulling you towards them.

2. When things don't go as you would like, focus on the positive outcome you want, not the consequences that you don't.

3. Don't rely on others to help set your goals. Use them to fuel your own if they can, but don't let them deflate you if they can't see the big picture.

The BIG Learning

Ken spent the weekend getting out the notes that he made when he started the business. He re-wrote all the reasons WHY he had wanted to start a business on big bits of paper and stuck them all over the walls of his home office. He got Jane involved and she was pleased to see the fight back in him. By the Sunday, Ken was clear that there was only one option and that was to make it work or go down fighting. Jane gave him her 100% support and would back him all the way.

On the drive to work, Ken's enthusiasm waned a little. He was still sure that keeping going was the best option, but he wasn't sure how he was going to get out of the mess he was in, and what he should do first. He also knew that something had to change in the business if they were going to make it work in the timescale that they had; he was just unsure what and where to start.

As he was about to pay for his petrol at the garage, he noticed an old, slightly battered business card in his wallet. It was Brad's, the guy he had met in Disney World. He had obviously put it there after the meeting and paid no attention to it since. Ken must have been drawn to it as a result of the happenings over the weekend. He remembered that Brad had asked him to keep in touch, and let him know of his progress. That was three years ago and Ken had thought that Brad was probably being polite, so he had never thought to follow up with him. He debated for a while whether after such a length of time Brad would remember him, but then again, these were tough times, and even if he had no idea what to do, he felt that a bit of Australian/American positivity would do him the world of good. So he made a note to give Brad a call that evening when the time difference would not mean it was the middle of the night.

That evening he sat in front of the phone for over an hour, trying to figure out what to say, worried that Brad would reject his call, laugh at his predicament, have no interest in his story, and virtually every other negative thought that a person could have. Jane came in with a cup of tea. "Haven't you called him yet?" she tutted. "Just get on with it. You said he seemed like a nice guy and even if he doesn't remember you, surely he'll just be polite and you can wish him well and hang up."

He gave out a big sigh, picked up the phone and dialled the number. After a few strange sounding overseas rings, a young girl's voice came on the phone. "Hello, Addison speaking, how can I help you?" She sounded about five years old and Ken smiled at her attempted mature way of answering the phone. "Is Brad there please, Addison? Tell him it's Ken from England."

He heard the phone bang down and the young girl's footsteps run down the hall as she called, "Daddy, Daddy, it's for you, it's a man called Ben from Inkland", with a giggle.

Ken then heard bigger footsteps getting louder and finally the phone was picked up again. "Brad speaking, how can I help?"

Ken's heart was now firmly in his mouth. "Hi Brad, sorry to bother you, it's Ken (he made sure he pronounced the K firmly) from England. I met you in the cocktail bar in Disney World about three years ago, and you were kind enough to give me some advice on becoming a business owner, and said I should stay in touch."

He could sense Brad thinking back. "Ah, Ken, two kids, accountant, fed up with your job, thinking of buying a business."

"That's me," Ken said, relieved that there was some recognition.

"How you doing, buddy, did you take the big step?"

"Sure did, it's been a hell of a ride so far, just as you said it would be." Ken then took a few minutes to bring Brad up to date with what had happened.

"The fact is, though, Brad, I'm not sure if I am cut out to be a business owner. I was a darn good accountant but running a business is so different. This knockback has left me doubting my ability to get the business back on track; I don't think I can do it. So I was just hoping you could give me some pointers as you did back then."

"Sure I can Ken. It won't take long, cos what you are going through, every business owner goes through at some stage in their life. You see Henry Ford once said 'Whether you think you can or you think you can't you are probably right'. It's all about how you think that makes it work. I'll put it a slightly different way. Have you got a pen and a piece of paper handy?"

Ken had thought that he might need to take some notes, so he was prepared. "Yep, ready to go."

"OK, write this down...

Be X Do = Have

"I call this the formula for life success. See once you are clear what you want to HAVE in life, you have to BE the person who is going to achieve this and DO whatever it takes to get it.

"The challenge you are facing is that it is all too easy to lose sight of what you want to HAVE, you are not always sure of what you have to DO, and you have not yet become the person you need to BE.

"You have to change from who you were to who you need to be, and your belief system must change first. Successful entrepreneurs know that they will make mistakes, things will go wrong and they will fail. Vince Lombardi said 'It is not how many times you get knocked down but how many times you get back up that counts'.

"The trouble with your accountant mindset is that you hate making mistakes. You see them as a weakness and so do everything in your power to stop them happening. The problem is that this stops you changing and thus you go back to how you were."

Ken was furiously taking notes, and giving little grunts of agreement as he did so. Ken thought to himself, 'How in five minutes could this guy get right to the heart of my dilemma?'

"So let me ask you a simple question Ken." Brad slowed his speech, and Ken knew that he was not going to like answering the question straight away. "Since you bought the business how much more learning of how to run a business have you done, and who do you turn to for help to become the successful businessman you want to be?"

"Well, er, um." Ken thought about coming up with excuses but knew that Brad would see right through them, but he had to say something in his defence. "I've been so busy that I haven't had time to do anything, and I must say I had no real idea what I should be learning."

"I understand," Brad said with an empathetic tone to his voice. "Running your own business is tough. There are loads of roles you have to take on and there will always be stuff to do. But the most important person in your business is YOU, and as I learnt from Jim Rohn many years ago, 'you must work harder on yourself than you do on your business', because you need to be the best YOU that you can be."

Ken sighed. Deep down he knew that Brad was right. He had learnt so much in the first year of the business, especially when the previous owner Ray helped him, but to be honest the second and third years he had just done exactly the same as he had in year one, and whilst the business had grown, Ken was not sure any of that had been down specifically to what he had done. And now they had lost such a big chunk of their sales, he knew he had no new ideas on how to get this back. So change he must, learn he must, do something different he must.

"So where do I go to learn how to build a successful business, Brad? Back to university and do an MBA? You mentioned finding somebody to learn from. I suppose I had a mentor in Ray, the previous owner, but he is retired now and living abroad. Where do you find these people? What about you – would you help me?" Ken was just talking and the last sentence came out without him really thinking about what he was saying.

"All good questions Ken, but I am in America and can only help so far. I suggest you seek out the best person in your area, make sure they come highly recommended and that they have a background of growing businesses your size. Don't worry if they've not been involved with sign companies before; you need to learn about growing a business, not how to make signs.

"It's been great talking to you again, Ken, do keep me posted and next time don't wait so long to contact me, just remember to BE and DO the best you can."

Ken thanked him and wished him well. On putting down the telephone receiver Ken felt different. For the first time since he started the business he could see that he was just following in the tracks that thousands of other businessmen and women had travelled in the past.

Ken finally saw that he was actually on a rollercoaster; once he learnt how it worked he could perhaps start to enjoy the ride.

Lesson 9
Never stop learning

Herbert Spencer first used the phrase 'survival of the fittest' after reading Charles Darwin's *On the Origin of Species* – in his *Principles of Biology* (1863) – but the real meaning of the phrase is closer to 'survival of those who are better equipped to change'. Dinosaurs were not unfit, but they were not able to change sufficiently to survive radical climate change. Human beings are the only species to inhabit virtually every landmass on the planet. We have a unique ability to learn and change our behaviour to suit the environment in which we operate. However, we often get trapped into thinking that we know everything we need to know, when the reality is that we don't know what we don't know.

Confucius once said "a foolish man thinks he knows everything when in fact he knows nothing. Whereas a wise man knows he knows nothing so at least he knows one thing." The day we stop learning is the day we stop growing. However, the process of learning is difficult and it takes hard work to do it well. Just ask any child at school. It is always easier not to learn than it is to learn. That is why it is so important to have empowering goals which you are working towards. Without them you would have to ask "Why bother?"

In the 1970s, Noel Burch from Gordon Training International developed the theory of 'Four Stages for Learning Any New Skill', which clearly shows the challenges we face whilst learning. Let me explain a little further.

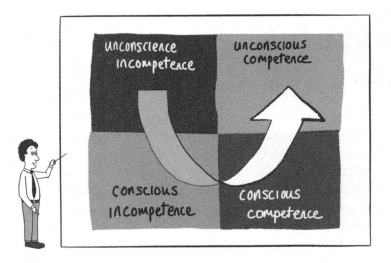

Unconscious incompetence

The individual does not understand or know how to do something and does not necessarily recognise the deficit. They may deny the usefulness of the skill or be blissfully unaware. In order to move out of this stage the individual must either recognise their own incompetence, or have it shown to them by another person or situation. The length of time an individual spends in this stage depends on the strength of the stimulus to learn.

Conscious incompetence

Once the individual is aware of their deficiencies they cannot go back to the previous level; you cannot unlearn something. The only choice you have is whether you do something to overcome the incompetence or stay where you are. Unfortunately, many people choose the latter and end up denying they have a problem, making excuses about why they cannot overcome it, or blame somebody else for the situation. In other words they become victims (see lesson 7).

Successful people, on the other hand, choose to take ownership of the situation. They know that it is their responsibility to do something about their incompetence, and are happy for others to hold them accountable in achieving their goals. These people become victors, as they choose to put the effort into moving to the next stage.

Conscious competence

This is the level of learning that is the hardest. The individual understands or knows how to do something; however, demonstrating the skill or knowledge to achieve the task requires concentration and effort. Mistakes are often made and actually are an integral part of the learning process. Napoleon Hill is quoted as saying: "No man ever achieved worthwhile success who did not, at one time or other, find himself with at least one foot hanging well over the brink of failure."

It is the transition from this stage to the next that separates the successful from the unsuccessful, the 'wheat from the chaff'. You have to be dedicated to the cause to put in the time to learn and become a master at what you do.

Malcolm Gladwell, in his book *Outliers*, believes that it takes 10,000 hours to truly master a skill, which is the equivalent to five years of total focus. Then to stay at the top of your game, you have to continue to have this level of dedication. Just look at the training that any top athlete puts themselves through in order to continue to win.

The challenge, just like the last level, is that it is easier to quit than it is to do what is necessary but, for those few that do, the next level awaits.

Unconscious competence

Once a skill is mastered, the task has become 'second nature' and can be performed at a subconscious level easily. As a result, the skill can often be performed while executing another task. At this point the individual normally looks back and wonders why they felt it was so tough getting there. Just look back at your own experience of learning to drive a car.

The challenge now, though, is that there is no challenge. The task has become easy and unless the individual keeps improving, the skill can become boring and meaningless, often leading to silly or reckless mistakes. Again, look at the daft things that people do once they have been driving for many years.

The reality however, is that the circle is now almost complete, because we have come back to where we started, at the unconscious incompetence stage. We have become so competent at the skill we were learning that we do not see there is another level waiting for us, if only we were to push on.

And push on we must because the key factor in understanding the four stages of learning is that to choose to remain at any one level is dangerous, and will cause us to go back to blame, excuses or denial. What gives us a sense of purpose and enjoyment in life is moving from one box to another, and herein lies the reason why successful people take on coaches to help them.

Not only can they learn quicker from somebody with the experience in what they are doing, but they have somebody to drive them, keep them focused, support them and ultimately to hold them account-able, and this is exactly what Ken was after.

BIG Actions

1. Whatever you want to be better at, always be studying. Read, listen to CDs, watch videos and attend courses.

2. Carry out a personal appraisal on yourself or get somebody to do it for you. Review your own BE x DO = HAVE formula and see which area needs work.

3. Seek an advisor to help you and always be asking for help on what you don't know.

The BIG Choice

After the call with Brad, Ken hit the internet straight away and looked up as much as he could on business advisors. As he had feared, there were quite a few and it was very difficult to distinguish between them. There were consultants, trainers, coaches, mentors and even therapists.

He started a list of possibilities, but thought that Brad was right when he had said recommendation would be the best way. He just wasn't sure who to ask. Nobody he knew was working with one, so perhaps his accountant or bank manager might know of other clients using them.

The next day he called his bank manager, Steve. After the pleasantries he asked, "Steve, I'm looking for a business advisor to help me take the business forward; do any of your clients work with one?"

"I'm not sure, Ken. I can ask around, but I thought with your experience you wouldn't need somebody to help. Is everything OK? You know you can always talk to me."

Ken pondered on this for a few seconds. Steve was very experienced; he had been a bank manager for 30 years, and Ken had known him in his previous job. He had moved his account to Steve after the first year when Ray's bank manager had failed to build any relationship with him during the first year of owning the sign company.

However, it just did not feel right opening up to Steve. After all, he was the one who had granted him the extra loan and overdraft, so having him as an advisor would surely be a conflict of interest. Also, Steve was an employee of the bank, and had never run a business, let alone built one, so Ken was not sure he would know enough to help him through this current set of challenges.

"Thanks for that Steve. I appreciate your offer of help but you're a busy man and I feel I need somebody who is qualified in doing this and can give me the professional attention I need. If you can have a look around for me and if somebody comes up, please let me know."

The next person Ken turned to was his accountant, Brian. He had known Brian for years, having been on many courses with him when he was a finance director. When he started the business it had been a no-brainer to take on Brian's firm to look after the accounts and tax affairs of Ray Signs, and he had been very impressed with the support Brian had given to him since then.

They would meet once a quarter to review the management figures, and Brian was very proactive in the advice he would give on tax and financial planning. They played golf together occasionally and Ken had always been impressed by Brian's business mind, as he was always able to come up with a good viewpoint, even if Ken did not always agree with it.

He decided to take Brian out for a game of golf to talk it through with him. Although Steve would not have been right, he thought that Brian might actually be a good mentor due to his more varied business knowledge, and the fact that he was a partner in his own business and therefore would be thinking more like a business owner than an employee.

After the round of golf, they sat outside in the late afternoon sun with a couple of pints of shandy, and Ken popped the question.

"So Brian, what I need is a business advisor to help me take the business to the next level. I know the potential is there and I have run it well for the last few years, but there are things I don't know and these are holding me back. I wondered if you would be up for the role."

"Well, let me start by saying that I'm really flattered that you thought to ask me, Ken. Thirty years of being in business and working with them has given me some great strengths, and I love helping businesses, so there is part of me that would love to take on the role." Brian took a long refreshing sip of his drink.

"However, you are not the first person who has asked me, and I have tried to do it twice before. On one occasion I bought into a business as a minority shareholder and thought I could support the owner that way. The trouble was that we wanted different things from the business. I saw it as an investment; he saw it as a way of life. I got so frustrated that after six months we decided to part company and only just salvaged our personal relationship afterwards.

"On the second occasion I did it as an extension of the accounts function; it was more of an external finance director role. We met on a monthly basis and I happily gave my support and threw in new ideas."

"How did that relationship work out, Brian?" Ken interjected.

"Very well actually, I still carry out the role and the business is ticking along fine. However, from what you have just said I don't think that my skill set is what you need right now. You have all the financial acumen you need. There are not many businesses on my books that keep their accounts to the standard you do, so I am not going to add much to that.

"Your plans are all about growth, sales, marketing and building a team and I must be honest with you, these things accountants are not the best at, and it would be wrong of me to say I could do it. I am more than happy to be a sounding board and perhaps meet with you a bit more often, but time wise I would struggle to do this more than monthly."

"What about one of your friends; I thought that you had a good mix when I came to your Christmas party last year?"

Ken responded, "I have thought about them, but part of the problem is that like you, they don't have the business knowledge that I need and even if they did, they are my friends. It would feel strange to have them working in the business with me and if it didn't work, you said it yourself, this would put a strain on our relationship, especially if I had to sack them."

Then Ken's face changed, his eyebrows went up, and he almost squeaked. "Hang on a minute, my friend Julie's boss is an entrepreneur who seems to have worked out how to run a successful business. I could ask him! At least I know he is where I want to be in a few years."

"Great idea!" Brian replied, almost as excited as Ken. "Why don't you give her a call and get some details."

Ken grabbed his mobile from his pocket and rang Julie. "Hi Julie, Ken here, how are you doing?"

After a couple of minutes of pleasantries, Ken asked the question that had been burning on his lips since he picked up the phone. "You know you said your boss might be up for helping me? Do you think that he still might and, if so, could you give me his details so I can give him a ring?" Ken blurted this out like an overzealous schoolboy.

"I'm sure he'll be happy to meet with you for a coffee and give you some advice. I know he's back in the UK for the next couple of weeks. Have you got a pen?" Julie said, totally unaffected by Ken's excitement.

Ken scrabbled around in his pocket and pulled out his golf score-card and pencil. "Yep, let me have it."

"Carl Edmundson", Julie said, then proceeded to spell it out letter by letter, followed by his mobile number. "The Company is CE Electrical. Give me a day and I'll either see him or drop him an email and say you'll be calling."

"That's brilliant, Julie, many thanks for that, see you at the pub on Friday." Ken ended the call and repeated the name and company to Brian with a big grin on his face.

Brian smiled back. "Did you say Carl Edmundson, CE Electrical?"

"Sure did, do you know him?" Ken was intrigued.

"Yes, for about 10 years. We have been his accountants and he's done very well for himself, so I can see why Julie would recommend him. My partner deals with his affairs and now you come to mention it I am sure that he works with an advisor of some description. It's a small old world." Brian took a long swig from his pint glass and smacked his lips in recognition of his drink's thirst-quenching properties.

"I tell you what, I'll email him as well, and with two people recommending he speaks to you I am sure it will happen. I also know that he's a golfer too so we could always arrange another round."

On that note both Ken and Brian finished their drinks, shook hands and made their way back to the car park.

A day later Ken called the number Julie had given him. He was a little disappointed when it went straight to voicemail, but Ken resigned himself to the fact that successful people like Carl probably filter all their calls to save time and effort, and left a brief message referring to Julie and Brian.

Ken was therefore a little surprised that about 30 minutes later his mobile rang showing the number he had just dialled.

"Ken speaking, is that Carl?"

"Yes it is, hello Ken, I've been hearing a lot about you from Julie and Brian, must be serious if two people say I should call you." Carl had a slight Yorkshire accent, but his voice seemed very calm and relaxed, not like Ken's would have been if a stranger had called him in the middle of the day.

Ken gave Carl a potted history of where he was and what he was looking for. "So I just wondered if you might be that person or if you knew of anybody who would fit the bill."

"Thanks for that Ken. So let me summarise. You have been in business for three years and you have pretty much exhausted your knowledge of what to do to grow any further. The setback with the lost contract means you need to do something now, but you do have a few months to get things going." Carl was unflustered and spoke slowly, as if he was thinking and speaking at the same time.

"Well let me start with the bad news. It's not me that you want. I love business and while I think I'm good at it, I do not have the patience to mentor you or the skill to pass on what I have learnt.

"What you need is a professional, Ken. Somebody who does this for a living, with an excellent track record, and a proven business growth model that even my simple brain can understand.

"You want somebody who can teach you the theory and help you put it into practice, who can keep you focused and provide account-ability each and every week. But above all you need somebody who is going to give you a positive return on your investment with them. And this is where I can give you the good news. I know just the guy who can help!"

"That's brilliant Carl!" Ken was over the moon – finally a recommen-dation. "Who is he?"

"His name is Kevin Williams, but I call him Coach Kev. He has been my coach for the last seven years and I consider him as being one of the main reasons I have been able to build a business that can work without me. Brian tells me that you play golf so let me arrange a game for this Friday afternoon. Kevin loves his golf so it won't be a hard sell. I'll text you the time and location. See you then." Carl was totally polite but straight to the point, clearly not wanting to waste a minute in superfluous chit-chat.

"That would be great Carl, looking forward to it." Ken was ecstatic that finally he could have found somebody to sit by his side on his rollercoaster journey.

Lesson 10
Choose your advisor wisely

Like many things in life there is no set way to be successful. Some people manage to make it with no outside help at all, others like to have many advisors, but one thing is certain: everybody could do a little better if they had help from the right source.

When looking for an advisor to help you, it is good to know what you are looking for. In my experience there are four main types of advisors, who come at things from different angles. Knowing which is best for you will help ensure you are in control and get the best return on your investment of time, effort and money.

Trainers and teachers

Trainers and teachers are great at imparting their knowledge and skills to other people. They may not have the real life experiences, but they have studied their topic for years and know it inside out. The best teachers are those who understand how their students learn and adjust their style to suit.

Some people learn through what they see (visual learners) and thus pictures, drawings and live demonstrations are best. Others learn from what they hear (auditory learners), so clarity of voice and eloquence of articulation is key. Others learn by doing (kinaesthetic learners), so hands-on, practical demonstrations and trial and error work best for these people.

If you want to know what will work best for you, think back to when you were at school and what teachers and lessons you preferred or hated. These will give you clues as to how you like to learn.

Mentors

Mentors are people who have 'been there, done it and got the t-shirt'. They have loads of practical experience, have learnt the lessons, often the hard way, and love to share these with their pupils. Mentors are great if you are following in their footsteps and you have total respect for what they have achieved. This is why so many people put themselves forward to be Alan Sugar's apprentice in the BBC TV series of the same name, or take on dragons in *Dragons' Den*.

Mentors tend to be very busy people, so your time with them will be brief. Make sure you are prepared every time you meet with them and have your questions ready.

Consultants

Consultants have got a bit of a bad reputation over the last few years. There were thousands of them in the 1980s and 1990s, used by businesses to great effect. Using a combination of teaching and mentorship with a hands-on approach, consultants are great at seeing and fixing problems. Because of their in-depth knowledge of an area they can get to the root of the issue and tell you exactly what to do to fix it. Think Gordon Ramsay in his TV series *Kitchen Nightmares*. Fly in, fix it, fly out again.

The problem with consultants is that once they have gone, the people in the organisation often revert to what they did before, wasting the time and effort put in by all. Only use a consultant if you are going to listen to what they say, take action and see it through.

Therapists

You might ask why you would ever need a therapist or psychologist when you run a business. Well the reality is that you would be mad not to consider it. I cannot remember or find out who said "therapy is wasted on the insane; it is the sane people who need it the most".

We all have issues that are easier to bury deep in our subconscious rather than face them, as I will reveal in lesson 11. These form our identity and while they can define us in a positive way, they can do the same in a negative way. The human brain is a very complex organ and to this day is not fully understood even by those that have studied it all their life. But without question psychologists are best placed to help us overcome those inner fears and issues that hold us back.

Coaches

Coaching is a relatively new term, especially in business, but has in fact been around longer than any of the others. If you go back to the formula of life success that Brad talked about, BE x DO = HAVE, and put the BE and DO on either end of the spectrum, consultants, mentors and teachers are very much about helping you DO things while therapy is 100% helping you BE a better person. Coaching covers the spectrum from BE to DO, and it is for this reason that in the sporting world if you don't have a coach you are not taken seriously as a sportsperson. In fact so important is it now that teams and athletes have specific coaches for specific parts of their game.

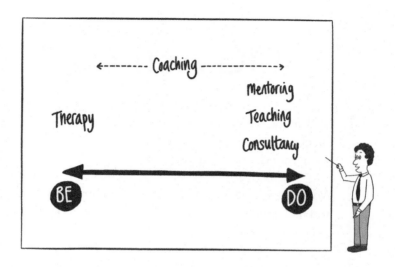

BIG Actions

1. Look at the types of businesses and people advisors have coached in the past and make sure you ask around for recommendations and testimonials.

2. Work out what type of advisor suits your style the best and make it clear to them what it is you want from them; after all it is in your interest to make it work.

3. If possible see them in action first and make sure you meet them a couple of times before deciding, but remember that, like all good relationships, yours will improve over time.

The BIG Change

I t was a bright sunny day when Ken pulled into the golf club. It was a very posh club, one that Ken had heard about but had never been lucky enough to be invited to before. There was a very long drive which ended at an ornate gate with a security guard in a little white hut. "Good morning sir, how are you today?" The guard smiled as he bent down to look in the car window.

"I'm great thanks. I'm here to play golf with Carl."

"Ah you must be Ken, we are expecting you. I'll open the gate for you, and if you drive to the main entrance the guys will look after you."

Ken was impressed by the customer service here. From that moment on he was treated like royalty, from parking his car, to carrying his clubs, to having his own named locker and clubs taken to the first tee. He made a mental note that none of this actually cost a penny apart from having great people and great training. There were a few things he could learn for his business.

Ken was ushered through to the bar where Carl, Kevin, and Brian were drinking coffee. They went through the normal introductions and pleasantries and then hit the golf course. Ken had thought about how to play the first meeting, and came to the conclusion that he would just use it as an opportunity to see if they got on. He did not want to scrutinise or be scrutinised today, but he did want to find out how the coaching relationship had worked between Carl and Kevin and what they got out of it.

On the 4th hole both he and Carl sliced their drives into the rough while Kevin's drive was straight down the middle. As they walked to their balls, Ken felt he had built up enough rapport to ask Carl his first question. "Carl, what made you take on a coach, and why did you choose Kevin?"

"Interesting question, Ken, and while it was quite a few years ago, the reason is as clear as it was then. I had been in business for five years and in first three years I had got to a nice level where it was providing a good profit, but I was working my socks off to keep it there. The next two years I was working as hard as ever but we grew very little. I knew that while I was a great electrician, I was not a great businessman, so I decided I needed to learn.

"I had met Kevin networking a few months earlier and he had invited me to an event he was running on how to grow and exit your business. Everything he talked about was bang on where I was and I met with him the next day and started coaching the following week. That was nearly seven years ago and I haven't looked back since." They found their balls in the semi-rough and soon rejoined Kevin on the green.

A couple of holes later Ken had another chance to speak to Carl alone. "Seven years seems quite a long time to be coached. Why has it taken so long?" Ken asked as they walked down the 7th, whilst Kevin was looking for his ball in the bushes.

"Strangely I have never seen our relationship as one with a time frame. I want to grow the business and push forward, Kevin helps me do that and I suppose when I stop wanting that I will stop needing Kevin. What you have to realise is that our relationship has changed many times over the years.

"When I started I just wanted to learn, so Kevin was more of an educator, teaching me all the areas of business that I did not know. After that I had to implement these skills, so Kevin helped me with feedback, problem solving and support when things were not going to plan. Finally when I got good and felt I was there, Kevin would challenge my decisions and help me see alternatives that once again I did not know I did not know, and so we keep moving forward at a higher and higher level."

Ken was starting to get a much better understanding of the coaching process, and although he had had time to find out a bit about Kevin from Carl, over the last few holes, he felt that he now needed to go a bit deeper as to what Kevin could offer him.

His opportunity to talk to Kevin came on the 16th, a long par 5 over water, which Carl had failed to drive and so had to go to the other side of the pond to drop and play up to their position.

"I'm getting from Carl that the key to unlocking the best out of coaching is to have a good two way relationship. What are you looking for in your clients, Kevin?"

"That's a really good way to put it, Ken. Carl's a really good case in point when it comes to what makes a good coaching client. The first attribute is that they have got to be hungry for success; if achieving goals is a nice to have rather than a must have, then it makes it diffi-cult for me to drive that person. Without a desire to be successful they are not prepared to do the hard work to get there, and I usually find these people give up after three months or so and go back to the way they were.

"The second attribute is a willingness to learn. I have a great little saying: the more you learn, the more you earn. The most successful people I know are all avid readers and never think they know it all. They invest more in their own education than many people get paid.

"The third is that if they say they are going to do something they do it. While part of my role is to keep them accountable, I am not their mother and I am not going to send them to their room if they don't get things done. I act as an external mirror of their conscience. When they promise something to me they are just verbalising an internal function, which reinforces their subconscious. I call this IVVM, which stands for

Idealise

Visualise

Verbalise

Materialise.

"I help with the formulating of the idea; getting Carl to visualise the outcome and then by verbalising it to me it ensures the best chance of materialising," Kevin replied.

"Hope you're not talking about me!" Carl had finally joined them after putting another ball into the water.

"That visualisation technique you taught me really does work. The only thing I could think about back there was don't put the ball in the water again, and lo and behold, my thoughts came to be." They all laughed and finished their round with high spirits and scores.

The 19th hole beckoned them in, and over a cold beer Ken put forward his final question. "Carl, what has been the biggest impact of being coached over the last seven years?"

As the question was asked Carl had his pint glass in his hand. He banged it down onto the table rather too heavily, causing the foamy beer to slosh out. "Sorry about that," he said while mopping up the fizzing mess.

"I look at my life in business as a journey of self-development in which I have had to grow at each level before I was good enough to move to the next one.

"At the start I was at school so I was a student, where I had to learn how to learn. I also learnt how to meet deadlines and how to prioritise my day in order to get all my work done. Then when I got my first job I had to learn a new set of skills, such as how to take orders and serve other people. I think I was quite lucky back then because I had some great bosses who I learnt a lot of management skills from, so that gave me the confidence to start out on my own.

"Starting a business from scratch was a case of learning by trial and error and the lessons got harder and harder. At this point I was on my own with nobody to learn from. I sort of got to the next level of being a manager of my own business, but as I told you before it was more out of blood, sweat and tears than really knowing what I was doing.

"I think that, like sport, you can get to a certain level on your own. A lucky few will make it all the way with very little coaching. But these guys are the exception. Most of us need help.

"Being coached really helped me change my behaviour from being an electrician running a business to a business owner running an electrical company. Some of this change was really hard and I did feel like going back to my old ways many times, but I knew that I was better than that, and so with Kevin's help I now see myself as a business owner and we are currently working on me moving to the next level of becoming an investor and growing my property portfolio and buying up a few other businesses to make CE one of the biggest in the area.

"Ultimately I might like to become a true entrepreneur and have multiple businesses and buy, build and sell them for the fun of it. But for now the goal is to sell this business and put enough money aside in property and shares so that I can be truly financially free and not HAVE to work again. I will then have a year or so off to enjoy things, and then decide if I want to move on to that final level."

Ken had been on the edge of his seat the entire time that Carl had been speaking. He so resonated with his story, even though they had come into business from completely different directions. Ken knew that he wanted to learn to become a true business owner and felt that Kevin could be just the coach to help him get there.

They drained their glasses and walked out to the car park. "Thanks for a good day," Ken said, shaking hands with each of them a little too vigorously.

"Kevin, I would be very interested in meeting with you to see what you think about the potential in my business and if we could work together." Ken got out his business card and swapped his for one of Kevin's.

"That would be great Ken; I'll get some dates and times over to you tomorrow. Safe trip home."

Ken left the golf club on a high; he had had a nice game of golf, learnt something new, and found himself a business coach to help him move the business forward. The rollercoaster was to take a change of direction again, but this time for the better.

Lesson 11
Change your behaviour

Human beings are like icebergs; what you see on the surface is a tiny percentage of what truly makes us up, and although we all have unique physical and genetic traits, most of how we behave is learnt.

As we grow we often have to change our behaviour to suit our new position in life. The problem is that the older we get the harder it is to change.

Kids have no trouble in changing as they grow up, mainly because their true identity is still forming and they have not got too many bad habits or limiting beliefs that hold them back.

The challenge is that the older we get, the more formed our 'iceberg' is, and the harder it is to change, so our behaviour does not always change with the new role that we find ourselves in.

So let's look at our 'Identity Iceberg' in the diagram. First you will notice that, like the tip of the iceberg, what we see is only a tiny percentage of what is underneath the surface. All we see of a person is their behaviour, but it is these behaviours that drive our actions and decisions and ultimately give us the results that we are getting.

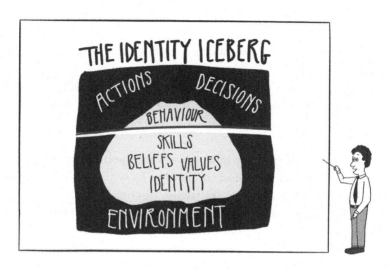

If these behaviours are working well and we are getting the result we want then all is good, but if not then we need to change these behaviours. However, as mentioned above, for many this is not as easy as it would seem.

In order to change these behaviours we must look below the water line, and at each level down it becomes harder and harder to change.

The starting point should always be our environment, because normally this is the easiest thing to change. If children are behaving badly when they are around certain other children, separating them will automatically change their behaviour. The same is true with you at work. If you are not getting things done in a busy open plan office, going to a room by yourself will allow you to calm down and become more focused.

If changing the environment has no impact on your behaviour then you have to look at the next level down and ask, "Do I have the skills and knowledge to change?" If not then you simply need to learn those skills, read a book, attend a course, or ask somebody. This is why, as I said in the last chapter, constant learning is so important.

However, having the skill and knowledge is sometimes not enough. Just look at smokers; they may know that smoking will kill them, but they don't change their behaviour and quit.

The next level down is your beliefs that your current behaviour is not helpful and you need to change. Now this level happens a lot with people who are not self-aware or choose to be below the line (lesson 7). It is not until this belief is challenged that they realise that they need to change. Back to our smokers, the government's tactic to help people quit is to put 'Smoking kills' on every packet, and now pictures of diseased organs, to challenge smokers' beliefs that smoking is not going to affect them.

Now most beliefs are relatively easily challenged with facts and just being aware that there are alternatives. However, some beliefs are so ingrained over years that they become our core values and it is only something major that can overcome these. For our smoker this is often a health scare, the death of a relative/friend, or the arrival of children, where they realise that they value other things more than their cigarettes and even themselves.

If none of these things change somebody's behaviour, then the only thing left that is stopping them is that their bad behaviour is such a major part of their identity that the thought of changing makes them feel that they will no longer be themselves.

This is why most smokers don't quit. It's not that they are addicted to nicotine, but that they are addicted to the identity of being a smoker, and at a subconscious level they like that identity. The only way to change at this level is cognitive therapy, which is why there is such a need for psychotherapists.

Luckily for Ken he has realised that his behaviour over the last few years has been responsible to a large degree for his current position and he is open to finding a coach to help him build on his skills and challenge his limiting beliefs.

BIG Actions

1. Find somebody to challenge your beliefs. You do not have to agree with them, but it will mean you are constantly looking for ways to improve.

2. Work on improving your identity by writing a dozen positive 'I am' statements and reading them to yourself every day.

3. Make a list of your core values and ensure that they are conducive to who you want to be.

The BIG Goal

Ken and Kevin had arranged a date for their first meeting a week later, and in the meantime Kevin had given Ken an envelope in which was Ken's homework to review with Jane in preparation. Kevin had asked them to set aside at least half a day of uninterruptable time, so that they could give it all their attention.

It had been over 20 years since he had last been given homework, when he was studying for his accountancy exams, and he was not sure how to take it. When he got home that evening he mentioned it to Jane and asked if she thought it a little odd that a man of his age had 'homework' to do?

"I think it's a good thing. It will give you something to focus on. You know you always work better when you have a clear task to do and a bit of pressure to get it done by a certain time. Just remember you are doing it for you not him."

This made sense to Ken. It was always good to hear somebody else give some positive affirmation that his course of direction was correct. They agreed to go to one of their favourite hotels for lunch on Saturday, so that they could arrive early to make a start, have a lovely meal and finish in the afternoon. That way they would not be disturbed and would be nice and relaxed.

They decided to have a look at the document before the Saturday, so that they could start thinking about the questions. He was quite surprised when he found that the envelope only contained five pieces of paper with a question at the top of each one and the rest were blank pages, presumably for them to write their answers.

The first question was:

Make a list of all the things in your life that cause you pain, frustration or make you unhappy, and that you don't want to experience in your business and personal life anymore (e.g. I don't want to work weekends or long hours).

The second question was:

Make a list of the 101 things that you want to have, experience, or do before you die, if money and time were not an issue (e.g. travel the world staying in five-star hotels).

The third question was:

You have now achieved all the things on the previous lists. Who else would you now help and what kind of legacy would you like to leave behind (e.g. build a school in Africa)?

Ken stopped after the first three pages and looked at Jane with a stunned expression on his face. "Well this is not going to be as easy as I first thought. I can think of a few things but are we going to be able to fill a page?"

Jane was her usual positive self. "I wouldn't worry about it now. Let's just keep it in the back of our minds and see what comes out on Saturday. What are the last two questions?"

Ken turned the page.

Imagine in 10 years you have built the business to its ultimate size and shape. At that point what would be its:

> *Sales*
> *Gross profit*
> *Overheads*
> *Net profit*
> *Number of employees?*

Now, imagine you have a time machine and can go forward 10 years to visit your business. In as much detail as you can, describe what the business looks, feels and sounds like.

Jane smiled when she heard this question. "Well that one is down to you. I'll focus on what we are going to spend the money on."

They both laughed and while Ken felt a little apprehensive about what this process would uncover with Jane and himself, he was very excited about finding out what their real wants and desires were.

Ken managed to find some time before the Saturday 'away day' to work on the figures. He felt that the business had the potential to reach £2m in sales revenues with a 60% gross profit and 20% net profit, which would give £400,000 profits each year, 1/3 on tax, and 1/3 to reinvest should leave him £100,000 to £200,000 income. Then when he came to sell, a minimum sale value multiple of three times pre-tax profits should give them just over £1m to retire on, more if they could find a good buyer.

Just doing this exercise had been a revelation to Ken. He normally spent his time at the office worrying about paying the bills and keeping in the overdraft limit. This was never energising, in fact quite the opposite, but now he could see what he was really driving towards; he finally had a big goal to work towards, even if he had no idea how he was going to get there.

Saturday came around rather quickly that week and Ken and Jane headed off to the hotel. They had purposefully not discussed the homework before, and both were keen to know what the other thought. They found a nice quiet part of the hotel, ordered coffee, got out the papers and looked at each other blankly.

"Well?" Jane said, intrigued at what Ken had come up with.

Ken passed the baton back to Jane. "What have you got?"

"I asked first," Jane responded, knowing that this was a battle he could not win.

"To be honest I don't know where to start; I've been thinking on this since we saw the question and I feel really ashamed that I don't know the answer. The business side of things was much easier, but what I really want to get from life personally I have no idea. I was hoping that you had more imagination."

"Thank goodness for that," Jane sighed with relief. "I thought I was a freak not knowing what I wanted in life. It has always been about you and the kids; I have never really stopped to think about me."

The coffee arrived at that moment and it gave them a well-timed pause. Ken was the first to speak when the waiter left.

"Well I suppose this is what the process is all about. If we don't know what we want in life then why would we do anything different to get there? Let's just go with the flow. Shout out whatever is on your mind, no right, no wrong, and let's see where we end up."

"You're on!" Jane perked up. "I'll start with what I don't want and I don't want you to work as much as you do. The kids are growing up fast and we have to make the most of the time they are with us."

"I won't argue with that." Ken took a bite of a biscuit and lost half of it down the sofa. "And I don't want you to have to sacrifice your social life looking after the kids all the time," he said whilst scrabbling to find the elusive biscuit.

It was a slow start, but the more things they wrote down, the more seemed to come out. It was as if they had put a mental dam in the way of all these things and now it was slowly breaking down.

The 'don't want' list was not that big, but the 'want' list kept on growing, from fast cars, to horses, to exotic places to visit, so much so that they ended up having to get more paper to write on. By the time they stopped for lunch they had written out three pages of 'wants', one page of 'don't wants' and three 'legacies'. They continued the discussion over lunch and with a couple of glasses of wine, the lists continued to be built in the afternoon.

By 4pm they were exhausted but euphoric. "We really should do this more often," Ken said, smiling. "It takes me back to when we got married and we had loads of dreams. Life's more exciting when you're moving towards something. Even if we don't achieve half of what we've written we'll have had so much fun getting there."

"Shall we make a night of it and get a room?" Jane suggested. "I'm sure your parents won't mind keeping the kids overnight." They looked at each other like teenagers and made the call to his parents. The rollercoaster had definitely taken an upturn.

Lesson 12
Select the right goals

As we saw in lesson 8, goals have a gravitational pull, and the bigger and clearer they are the stronger the pull towards them. Many have written about the importance of goal setting but nobody has really identified why this is so.

Whilst I am not a brain surgeon, psychologist, scientist or biologist, I have extensively studied goal setting and its power, and my conclusion is that there are three levels of goal setting which are intrinsically linked to the human brain.

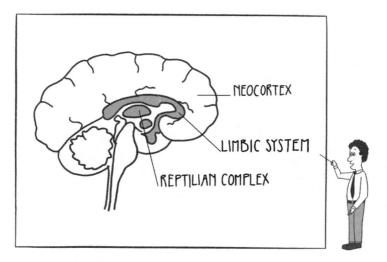

The oldest and most established part of our brain is the reptilian complex. We share this with all the other animals and it takes care of our basic survival functions of fight, flight, feeding and reproduction. It is there to keep us alive and as such is very powerful. It is also

133

the part of the brain that is most developed when we are first born. As soon as a baby comes into the world, the first thing it does is cry to get the attention of its mother. It does not think; it just does. Also think back to a time when you were in danger. Your instinct to survive comes naturally and very quickly, often surprising even you.

There is another interesting side effect of using this part of our brain. When we engage the reptilian brain certain chemicals are released that improve our performance, testosterone, endorphins and oxytocins. These naturally produced chemicals give us a feeling of energy, higher sense of alertness, and make us feel more alive. This is why we love taking risks, watching horror films and even going on rollercoasters at amusement parks.

In terms of goal setting the reptilian brain deals with the first level of goal setting, that of moving away from pain goals. These are goals that drive us away from what we do not want. Examples are: I do not want to be hungry, scared, homeless or lonely. For most people who start a business these goals get us up and running and provide the drive to do whatever is necessary to get our business to a point where it is safe.

We do not have to make plans or give these goals much thought. If we think we are in pain or in danger then we just get on with it. However, just like a horse that will run and run to get away from perceived danger, this part of the brain has no real sense of direction; it will just keep going until it is safe and then it will switch off.

So what happens once a business owner achieves their level one goals to get themselves away from danger? Well, just like an animal that has managed to evade a predator, they stop, relax, and go back to working on the other two functions that this part of their brain looks after – eating or reproducing.

They will happily stay doing this until the next dangerous event comes into their life, when they will repeat the whole exercise. For humans we call this our comfort zone. This is our little patch of grass where we feel safe and secure. However, stay here too long and boredom and complacency set in. See lesson 1 for more on this.

Humans can also find constantly living using only this part of their brain very tiring, constantly on the lookout for danger and sometimes even subconsciously creating it so that they can get excited about running away again.

The lesson we must learn is that in order to move us out of our comfort zone and further away from pain, we have to engage the second level of our brain, namely the limbic system. This part of the brain controls our emotions, loves, wants and desires. So rather than focusing on what we do not want, this part of the brain works on what we do want. This is traditional goal setting as we know it. Set your sights on goals that motivate you, are exciting and help you move towards something that inspires you.

With these goals, the bigger the better and the only limit is that of your imagination. Herein lies the problem for most business owners. Because most business owners have spent a great deal of their business life moving away from pain, they have not sufficiently developed this part of their brain function. They have not stopped to work out exactly what they want to get from their business, what lifestyle they want to live, where they want to go on holiday, cars they want to own, the perfect house etc.

The fact is that every successful business person has become successful because that is what they wanted to achieve. They set BIG goals and went for it and just like 'move away from' goals, when they are working towards their 'want goals' the brain gives off the same chemicals making them feel motivated and alive and wanting to achieve even more.

The problem comes when we achieve all our want goals and we have everything that we set out to have, because we think there are no more goals to strive for. At this point we enter another comfort zone in which, if we stay there too long, just like the first comfort zone, we will get bored and complacent.

However, unlike before, because we now have so much we rarely slip directly back into pain and thus we stagnate and potentially become a below the line person (lesson 7).

You can see this with a lot of successful people who reach the pinnacle of their careers and then start to make stupid decisions such as taking undue risks, gambling, or having affairs, thus engaging the natural highs that come with the chemicals in the brain when we are in fight or flight mode. Alternatively they seek artificial highs that come from drugs and alcohol. Left unchecked, all of these can have the potential to leave the person in a desolate position, which iron-ically takes them back to engaging their reptilian brain once more.

What these people have not yet understood is that there is a third level of goal setting which comes from the final part of our brain development. The neocortex is where our rational and logical thought takes place. The René Descartes quote "I think therefore I am" sums up this part of the brain and separates us from all other animals on the planet. This is why humans philosophise on our purpose in life, our sense of life and death, our place in the universe and ultimately our spirituality.

So what sort of goal setting is this part of the brain responsible for and how can it move us out of the second comfort zone, once we have everything that we can desire? Well the answer is that once we have all we want and need then the only thing that can motivate us is not what we can do for ourselves, but what we can do for others.

This is why so many people find that helping others is far more rewarding than anything they did for themselves. Ensuring your kids get a great start to life and achieve more than you were able to; helping the less fortunate through charity work; mentoring, and teaching your team, are all ways that we can utilise our neocortex to have a sense of purpose that will last forever.

History is littered with successful people who have learnt the power of level three goal setting, from Andrew Carnegie and John D. Rockefeller in the late 1800s and early 1900s, right through to Richard Branson and Bill Gates in current times. All used level two goal setting to create immense wealth and then level three to continue to be motivated and do good for others.

Now there are some people who can transcend level one and two and go straight to level three. Mother Teresa and Nelson Mandela spring to mind, but they were very special individuals and had probably been exposed to unique circumstances that led to their 'calling'. For the rest of us, all we need to do is understand which level of goal setting is going to work for us and be happy where we are, safe in the knowledge that once we achieve the goals we set we can always set new ones, be it away from, towards, or for others.

Oh, one final lesson on goals. You may have heard about SMART goals: Specific, Measurable, Achievable, Realistic and Timely. Well I totally agree with these sorts of goals, but I do find that they can lead to quite dull and boring goals. If you make them Inspiring and Emotional then you turn them into SMARTIE goals and for those that remember the advert, "only Smarties have the answer"!

As for Ken, going back to WHY he was in business and WHAT he wanted to get out of it was fundamental to getting back his motivation and with it anything was again possible.

BIG Actions

1. Make a list of what you don't want in your life. Then rewrite them so they are positively stated.

   "I don't want to live in this house becomes I want to live in a house like………………"

2. Make a list of the 101 things you want to have or experience before you die and then find pictures depicting them to put onto a dream board, so you can see them every day.

3. Write your own epitaph. What will people say about what you did when you have passed? Remember the words of Henry Ford: "Whether you think you can or you think you can't, you will probably be right!"

The BIG
Plan

The day of the meeting came, and Ken had already decided to take Kevin on as his coach. He did, however, want to wait to commit until he was clear on what direction Kevin was going to take him in with the business.

Kevin asked Ken how the homework had gone, and Ken wondered if Kevin had noticed him blush as he answered. "It was really good. Hard to start with but once we got into the swing of things we could not stop." Ken placed the papers on the desk for Kevin to read.

"Excellent, and from this I see that the goal is £2m in sales revenue and £400,000 of profits in 10 years and there are some great personal goals here." Kevin continued to read the forms Ken had given him, muttering and smiling as he went.

"You have made a really good start on this. So before we go any further I'm going to give you an outline of how I like to run these sessions. First we are going to spend a little time reviewing these goals so I can make sure that they are really what you want to achieve. Then we will review where you are with the business right now and finally we will work on the strategies that will get you from one place to the other, and decide which ones we will focus on in the next 90 days."

Ken liked this approach, nice and simple with clear steps to complete. He was, however, a little apprehensive about what they might uncover. It felt a little like a medical examination when you know it is for the best, but you are just not sure what will be revealed.

Kevin kicked off. "What you have to understand is that businesses are like human beings, exactly the same on the inside but totally unique on the outside. So we are going to start by looking at the four areas that make up the DNA of all businesses.

1. Finance and administration – the way you record the transactions of the business

2. Sales and marketing – the way you generate sales

3. Operations – the way you take orders, produce and deliver your product/service

4. Team – the way your team perform

"I am going to ask you a number of questions around each of these areas, and I need you to be as honest with me as you can. Each area of weakness is actually an area of opportunity as we can improve it to get better results."

They spent the next three hours digging into the running of the business. Ken actually found it a cathartic experience, as he offloaded all of the problems of the business. There were times when he thought an area of the business was quite good, but when Kevin probed, he realised there was much room for improvement.

This was especially true around the finance side of the business. Being an accountant, Ken had always been proud of the fact that his accounts were up to date and accurate. The Maddison bad debt had shown that he had become sloppy and the systems were not as robust as they should have been. When Kevin asked him if he had an annual budget, weekly sales and production figures, product line margin reports, profitability per job and cashflow forecasts, Ken began to feel like he had been an idiot for not doing these. He had done them all in his finance director role, but then he had only had to focus on this; now he had so much more to do he never really found the time.

Not once did Kevin criticise or look down on Ken, especially around sales and marketing, where Ken really had little idea of what he was doing. Sales had always been the responsibility of his sales manager Nick, and Ken had very much left him to get on with it. When sales were down, Nick always had a reason, which Ken never quite believed, but had no way of disproving. When they were up, Ken gladly paid the commissions on the sales, but most of the time the results the following week were poor again, making production quite difficult to plan.

As for marketing, Ken thought advertising was a waste of time, having put adverts in papers with no return. They had a website, which generated the odd enquiry, but most were of poor quality and rarely led to new work. The growth over the last few years had mainly been as a result of networking and referrals, but there was no strategy around these; they just seemed to work.

The operational side of the business was generally better than the previous two areas. Quality was high, deliveries were on time and production efficient. Robert was a sound guy and somebody who Ken was happy to rely on. The only weakness that Kevin pointed out was that everything relied so heavily on Robert that if he was not there for more than a week, very little of the production could be done.

As a whole the team were OK, but the previous few weeks had highlighted how disconnected they were. Nick's sales team always seemed to be busy with no real results. Robert's operations team were young and undeveloped. Pam was a lovely older lady but hardly dynamic. On the whole the team were adequate but it was hardly an enjoyable or optimistic environment, especially since Ken's outburst a few weeks ago.

The three hours flew by, and by the end both Ken and Kevin had made copious notes on what the strengths and weaknesses of the business were.

"So the question is, Ken, would you like me to help you find the strategies to improve and grow your business and achieve your goals?"

Ken tried very hard to keep his cool. He had promised himself not to make a decision on the spot and to give himself time to think about it and review it with Jane. However, he totally understood what needed to happen and knew that without help it was not going to. The three hours with Kevin had been great and he had no qualms about having Kevin as his coach.

"I would love it if you would be my coach. When can we start?" Ken smiled and offered his hand as a way of sealing the deal.

Kevin gave it a firm shake and they spent a few more minutes reviewing the programmes and prices. After the paperwork had been signed, Kevin shook Ken's hand once more.

"Right, Ken," Kevin said as he put his pen away and tided up his papers. "Your homework over the next few days is to reflect on what we have been through today and make a note of anything else that comes up. Also I want you to do some market research to see how big the market for signs is in the area you want to cover. You say £2m turnover is your goal, but I want you to prove to me that this is doable with the competition you have."

"That sounds like a good idea, but where would I get that information?" Ken was looking a little perplexed.

"The best starting point is the number of businesses in the area that need signs and a summary of the sizes of your competitors. It does not need to be accurate, just an indication. If you have any queries, just give me a call.

"Oh and one last thing," Kevin said as he reached into his briefcase. "I would like you to read this book. It's one that I wrote called *Profit Builders*. It has a lot of the strategies that I think will be useful for growing your business and I want you to understand them so you can decide if we will use them.

"You will have to get used to reading as part of the programme. I need you to read at least one book a month, more if you can. After all, *the more your learn, the more you earn*."

A week later the second part of the meeting was held. This was where they would identify the strategies that Ken would use to turn the business round and take it to the £2m mark.

Ken had done many business plans before for banks and investors, but always been disappointed with their effectiveness. It seemed that once they were done they were put in a drawer and not referred to again. Even if they were, they were more a description of the destination rather than a road map of the journey.

Kevin arrived with a big roll of paper and a pile of Post-it notes. "Right Ken, this is planning the easy way. We are now going to go back over the four areas of the business and pick out the key strategies that we are going to use to move the business forward. This is just blue sky thinking at this stage; no time frames are involved. We are going to get it down, then get it right, focusing on what we need to do in the first 90 days to get you from chaos to control, then in the next year to build on that foundation, and then over 2–3 years on the systems and processes that will get you ready for exit."

"Now let's see the results of your homework." Kevin leant forward and cleared a space on the table for Ken to present his work.

Ken had been very busy preparing for this meeting, as well as reading the book Kevin had given him and making notes all over it. For the next few hours, Ken was in Post-it note heaven. He used different colours for different areas of the business, and laughed at himself when he realised that his attention to detail behaviour meant that every Post-it was in perfect alignment.

Kevin interspersed the meeting with examples and explanations of certain strategies that they could use to improve each of the four areas and Ken loved the education process. He could not remember when last he had spent so much time thinking about improving and growing his or anyone else's business.

By the end of the session, Ken was exhausted, but in his hand was a large poster-sized piece of paper covered with colourful Post-it notes, which in turn were covered with loads of writing.

"For your homework this week, I want you to review this plan and select the 13 strategies you want to complete in the next quarter. That will give you one per week. If you feel that one will take you longer than a week then break it down into the tasks that will take you a week. When you have this 90-day plan send it to me to review and at our first coaching session we will finalise it and get started on putting it into action." Kevin picked up his briefcase, put away the unused Post-it notes, and bade Ken a fond farewell.

Ken was very excited. For the first time in his business he knew where he was going and had the makings of a plan to get him there. He actually now felt HE was in control of the rollercoaster.

Lesson 13
Fail to plan, plan to fail

Winston Churchill is credited with this quote and it is so true. Anything important in life is planned: building a house, a wedding, birthday party; even baking a cake needs a plan (recipe). So why do so few businesses have proper plans?

Well the simple answer is that plans are important when there is a time frame that must be adhered to (organising a party or a wedding) or you want others to replicate the process (baking a cake or building a house). Most business owners do not view their business in either of these ways. They rarely say:

"I want to build my business to this level by this date" or

"I want to build a business that others can run for me."

They see the business as one in which they must react to the environment and deal with whatever is thrown at them. Now I am not saying that this approach will not work; after all you could jump in a boat and head out to sea with no plan of where you are going and maybe the wind and tide would take you to a lovely port in the Caribbean, but there is more chance it would leave you bobbing around in the sea or shipwrecked.

Understanding that you need a plan is not the problem. The problem comes from the fact that most business plans that are available to business people are not the right sort. In my experience there are three types of business plan and it is only the third type that is effective for helping business people steer their business to a safe and successful harbour.

Business Plan 1 – for the bank

Most people in business will have prepared one of these at some time and its sole purpose is to obtain funding from the bank in the form of a loan or overdraft. It is predominantly made up of numbers: profit and loss accounts, balance sheets, cashflow forecasts and maybe a little background information on the business and owners.

The banks are interested in two main things when they lend money: their security if you default and your ability to repay the loan and interest. They have no interest in your business strategy or how you are going to achieve these figures, only whether your track record is good enough and what you want the money for is not too risky.

Once a bank business plan is complete and the money has been received, I bet 99% of them go into a drawer and are never looked at again.

Business Plan 2 – for investors

Investor business plans will contain all the information of a bank plan, but as their purpose is to get an investor to buy into the business, they will have to contain a few additions.

Investors are less concerned about security and interest cover but what they want to see is a good return on investment in the form of profits and increase in share value. Business investors are also savvier and will want to know of external opportunities and threats and internal strengths and weaknesses. They will want a full market and competitor analysis, understanding of the business' Unique Selling Proposition (USP) and a financial risk analysis.

Investors do not just invest in the business but, more importantly, the people running the business, so profiles and psychometrics of the management team will be essential. Finally, this form of plan should show a clear exit strategy so that the investor is happy that they can move on when the time is right.

Unlike the banks, investors are more likely to keep referring to the business plan, to ensure that the business is on track and that the directors are performing to the required level. However, the plan is more of an overview of WHAT needs to be done rather than a plan of HOW it is to be done. Think of it like the picture on the box and the contents list of a model plane kit, rather than the instructions on how to build it.

For the instructions you need the third type of business plan.

Business Plan 3 – for the owner

If you think of the type of plan you would have if you were to build a house, go on a big trip, or have a wedding, you would not be far wrong.

You would have a detailed plan of what you needed to do each day, week and month. Each step you took and milestone achieved would be recorded and you would always know if you were in front or behind schedule, and if there were multiple people involved you would ensure accountability by having recorded who does what by when.

In comparison building a business is far more complicated than anything else I can think of and it will take more people a lot longer to complete. The final challenge is that all the other examples have a clear end game: house built, trip taken and wedding complete. A business is more of a moving target which is why you first need to create your own time frame and milestone goals.

Because this is going to be a working document, the time frame you choose must be appropriate. I find that 90-day plans work best. Probably because this time frame works with the natural seasons we are all used to. It is just far enough to not be in reactive reptilian brain mode but not too far that we have to make too many assumptions.

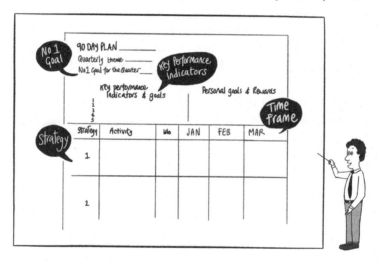

In your 90-day plan you should start with a theme for the quarter, just to give everybody an idea of what area you are focusing on. Next you need to clearly identify the number one goal you want to achieve for that period, and state this in a positive way. Then ascertain the key performance indicators you are going to use to track your performance. Finally you identify the strategies you are going to work on, breaking them down into activities that need to be completed, assigning those activities to the best people in your team, and then allocating a suitable time frame to each one.

All of this should be on one page if possible to keep it simple, and this document should be used on a weekly basis to keep track of what has been done and what needs to be planned in for completion that week. See the diagram for a good example.

Now Ken had his plan, in the words of Elvis Presley, all that was needed was "a little less conversation and a little more ACTION".

BIG Actions

1. Make time to spend a few days each year to review your successes over the last year and set your BIG goals and plans for the next 2–5 years.

2. Every quarter spend a day preparing your strategic 90-day plan and remember to set your SMARTIE goals.

3. At least once a week spend an hour reviewing your 90-day plan and booking into your diary the actions you need to take for the following week.

The BIG
Action

Ken had not told the team about his work with Kevin so far, but coming back to the office with a poster-sized wall chart was going to be difficult to hide. Since his outburst with Pam, the atmosphere with the team had not been good. Everybody was getting on with their jobs, but it was not a nice place to work.

Ken had done his homework for Kevin and squeezed in an extra session to review the 90-day plan and firm up on the strategies that he was going to start with. Doing this had made him realise that there was no way that he could implement the plan on his own and that getting the team on board to help him achieve the goals was paramount.

All this positive thinking with Kevin had given Ken far more energy than before and, while he was still apprehensive, he decided to bite the bullet and bring the team together and explain the situation. He called a meeting for 4pm that day, feeling that if it went wrong he could at least escape and have the night to sleep on it.

"Thanks for coming. First I'd like to apologise for my recent behaviour. As you know we were hit pretty hard by the loss of Maddison & Co, and my reaction was very emotional and not that helpful. The reality, though, is that we have a short-term issue that needs to be fixed, but more importantly we have a long-term future to secure."

Ken was looking at each of the team to see signs of engagement or whether they had already come to their own conclusions and switched off. He was pleased to see that they seemed to be with him so far.

"We have a great business here and we have huge potential to make it bigger and better. This setback might actually be looked back on as being the turning point of the business. It was perhaps the shock treatment that was needed to show me that being good is the biggest enemy of being great. For the last few years we have been drifting, doing OK but not headed anywhere." Ken was really getting into his stride.

"When I took on the business I wanted to build a business that we could all be proud of, one that was looked on as being one of the best in the area. And the last few months have made me realise that this is still the goal and we are going to realign ourselves to achieve this.

"To help us with this journey I have found us a top business coach. Just as a football team would seek out the best coach in the game to help them win the title, I have done the same to help us achieve our goals."

Ken then spent the next few minutes bringing the team up to date with what he had been working on, the £2m goal and how the 90-day plan would be used. The team were in no way against what he was saying but Ken did feel that they were treating him a little like he had just stepped off a space ship and was telling them about the aliens he had seen. 'No matter,' he thought, 'this is only the first day, and actions will speak louder than words.'

During the following weeks Ken was a man on a mission. Meeting with Kevin every week for their session entailed reviewing the previous week's wins and challenges, brainstorming ideas on how to implement that week's strategy and agreeing on the goals that Kevin would hold him accountable for next week.

In no way did Ken feel that he was working for Kevin; he was not his boss and he could part company with him at any time he liked, but he did have a sense of calm that he had somebody to report to and to feel he was sharing the ups and down with.

The end of the first 90 days came around too quickly. Kevin had arranged a half day, off site at a local hotel, for him and Ken to take stock and plan for the next quarter.

Ken arrived with his big wall chart that had the Post-it notes on it and a bit of a downbeat look on his face.

"Morning, Ken, what's up? You look like you've gotten out of the wrong side of the bed," said Kevin in his normal positive manner.

"Well, I was looking through the 90-day plan last night and then at the wall chart we did and we just don't seem to have done as much as I had hoped. I had 10 strategies to get done this quarter but I have only finished six of them, and just look at all that other stuff that we have to do." Ken slumped in his chair with the resignation of a beaten man.

"Where the hell did Mr Negative come from?" Kevin stood up and poured himself a coffee from the pot that the waiter had brought over a few minutes before.

"This is your perfectionist coming out again. Stop looking at the pint as half empty; let's look at it as half full. Now, drink this." Kevin thrust a cup of piping hot black coffee under Ken's nose. "And let's review what you *have* done."

They spent the best part of an hour reviewing the work that Ken had been completing over the quarter. The biggest success had been from the strategies they implemented to improve cashflow. The debtors had been reduced by simply getting the invoices and statements out on time and following up anybody who was a day overdue with a phone call. Ken had also managed to put his prices up on three types of work that were low in profit margins, which had been identified when they started to have key performance indicators for every job completed.

The result of these simple changes had put over £10,000 into the bank account, so the extra overdraft that they had got from the bank had hardly been touched.

The second area where massive progress had been made was Ken's time management. He had prepared himself a default diary that booked out time to work on his important but not urgent tasks and he kept a daily log of his time, which meant that he was rarely doing things that were not moving the business forward.

But the area that he was most pleased with was getting some simple systems and processes into the business so that the team were more effective. Kevin had asked Ken to calculate what saving this would have over a year and the figure had amazed Ken. That one simple strategy would pay for Kevin for the next three years, so in effect his coaching from this day forward would be FREE.

"There you go Ken. OK, I agree there is still a lot to do, but you have already made such a difference. You have to remember that the key to success in business is that it is a marathon not a sprint. Everybody overestimates what they can get done in a week, but underestimates what they can get done in a year." Kevin poured two fresh coffees and tucked into the biscuits.

"The other thing that you have missed is YOU! I think that you have grown in confidence and motivation every single week. That is why when you slumped into that chair I was so surprised. Don't worry that you get down occasionally. Running a business is very tiring and I know you've not had a break these last three months. So that is going at the top of the goal list for next quarter – a week away with Jane and the kids."

Ken smiled. He knew Kevin was right, but it was good to hear somebody giving him positive feedback and bigging him up. "Right, I am totally above the line now, pint glass full to the brim! Let's get planning on the next quarter!" Ken beamed a smile so big that Kevin thought his head would split in two.

The rhythm of weekly and quarterly meetings with Kevin continued for nearly five years. Ray Signs grew from strength to strength. In the first year Ken had replaced the entire income that they had lost from Maddison & Co and profits were up 20%. Year two saw the sales and marketing strategies they implemented at the end of year one come into play and the business nearly doubled in that time.

This rapid growth put some strain on Ken again, because the workforce had to double as well and this pushed Ken's newly learnt management skills to the test on many occasions. They still got a few things wrong. One bad recruit cost them a key contract and another good member of staff, but Ken no longer feared making mistakes. So long as he knew why they went wrong and what he could learn from it, then it was a price worth paying, because he rarely made the same mistake twice.

During those two years most of the original team left, and only Nick the operations manager remained. Ken never had to fire one of them; they either left because they knew they could not keep up or they just did not want to get out of their comfort zones and push themselves. Losing people never became a worry to Ken, because he always found that they were replaced with somebody better, who was clear on the goals and the values of the company.

Ken's home life also improved over the years. He managed to get his week's holiday in the second quarter, although he did have to phone into the office a few times, a fact he chose not to share with Kevin.

At the end of the first year he had booked his first two- week holiday back to Disney World with the kids, and since then he had taken as many holidays and long weekends as he wanted – which actually was not as many as he could have had.

By year three, the business was flying. Ken had brought some real talent into the business, pinching them from a competitor in the neighbouring town, which had been plodding along for a number of years. In fact it was one of the managers there who had asked Ken about coming to work for him, because he felt "they were going places and he wanted to be part of it".

Ken had asked Kevin to coach the top guys and help make them into business owners, because Ken was starting to see that they might have the ability to run the business fully without him and potentially organise a Management Buyout (MBO).

The £2m turnover came in year four, actually six months before Ken's original plan had stated. Ken was working 3–4 days a week, and frankly the team would rather have not had him around so that they could just get on with it.

Profits were more than Ken needed to live on, even after paying out good bonuses to the team, and for the last six months Ken had been working with Kevin on his investment portfolio of properties and stocks and shares, to give him some additional security and a passive income when he chose to stop.

It was a week before Ken's fifty-third birthday when the phone rang. It was Brian, his accountant, who sounded rather excited.

"Hi Ken, hope you are well, looking forward to seeing you and Jane next week, really appreciate the invite."

"You're welcome Brian; it wouldn't be the same without you. But I get the feeling this not what you're calling about. Have you been on the happy juice?"

"Bang on, Ken! I was going to do this all serious, but I am just too excited to do that. You know that we do the audit for Signs UK, the national sign company that you have been a pain in the side of for the last few years?"

Ken grunted in agreement, slightly confused about where this conversation was going.

"Well, I was doing the audit review with the managing director the other day, and your name came up. Once he knew we acted for you his eyes lit up and he asked me if you were for sale. Of course I said no, but that you were a businessman and as such anything might be possible."

Ken had sat down in his chair and taken a sip of cold coffee that nearly made him cough all over the phone. "AND ..." Ken drew the words out slowly.

"He said if you were, they had the cash and would love to meet you. What do you think?" Brian gasped for air, as if he had exhausted himself with this one sentence.

"That sounds promising," Ken said calmly, trying to hide the excitement that he was actually feeling. "I have nothing to lose as I don't have to sell to them, because I can carry on as I am or work towards the MBO we talked about. But if the offer is good enough then they might just set me up for life. Get it organised; does he play golf?"

Ken's rollercoaster was looking like it was coming to the final magnificent end of the ride.

Lesson 14
Life is a journey not a destination

The great Jim Rohn once said, "Don't become a millionaire for the money you will make; become a millionaire for the person you will become."

Many people who start their business do so because they have to make a living to support themselves and their family. They have no intention of becoming wealthy or using the business to achieve great things. Some see money as the root of all evil and the thought of having more than they need fills them with dread, so that subconsciously they will do everything in their power not to attract it. The problem with these people is that they will only ever create themselves a JOB and never achieve the full potential of themselves, their businesses or any of the people that work with them.

Money itself is not evil, nor will it make you happy. It is just an inanimate object, just as a gun on its own is not good or evil; it just depends on whose hands it is in and how it is used. What money will do is magnify the person you are. The more money you have the greater the magnification. If you are an unhappy person without money, with it, you will become a rich miserable person. Yes there will be things you can buy to cover up your unhappiness but deep down you will be little changed.

Think then of money as being the scoring system of business. Just as in any game you play, the higher the score the better you are doing, and you can either play to better your score every year or you can play to beat others. It just depends on how you like to play.

The key is that you have to enjoy playing the game, otherwise just having a big score is a little pointless. That way, even if you are not scoring so well, you can still enjoy playing the game. I used to often wonder why athletes would compete in events that they had no chance of winning. You see this in sport all the time: the Jamaican bobsleigh team, non-league football teams in the FA Cup, and the fancy dress runners in the London Marathon.

The fact is that there can only ever be one winner and if this were the only reason for competing, too many people would go away unhappy and never compete again. Also, winning is a very temporary affair. Just think about an Olympic athlete who trains for four years to win a gold medal, yet when they do so the moment is over in a flash. Many of the top athletes are straight back into training for the next Olympics within a few days.

The reason we compete in sport is that it is the competition that excites us. The pushing of our limits, having a focus on one goal, doing the best we can and seeing our improvement every time we play. If this is true in sport then it must also be true in business.

Unlike sport, business has no imposed endgame. There is no championship or gold medal to win, no time frame to work to, and as long as we are healthy we can compete up to a ripe old age. So goals must be set by the owner, as we saw in the previous chapter. However, one such ultimate goal could be imposed: that of the final sale of the business and the retirement of the owner.

In his book *The E-myth Revisited*, Michael Gerber suggests that every business should be built with an ultimate sale in mind; otherwise the owners are destined to be working IN the business forever.

Very few businesses are actually ever sold; most fail along the way, some are passed on for little consideration, but the lucky few sell and sometimes for amounts that set the owners up for life.

Sales are most likely to management teams or somebody like Ken when he started, although such people are unlikely to have much money.

Suppliers or customers will pay more if they see you as a strategic purchase, as was the case with Ken, or if you fit the bill then venture capitalists may be interested or the business could even be floated on the stock market, where mega sums can be made.

Just remember, though, that a sale is not the final destination; it is just another stopping point on the journey of life. You still have to find yourself another rollercoaster to master and enjoy riding, because after all where is the fun in standing still?

BIG Actions

1. Make sure you have options for who could buy your business and have a figure in mind as to what you would sell it for, and take it when it comes.

2. Know what value of assets you will need invested to provide you with a passive income when you wish to stop work.

3. Keep your own personal balance sheet that shows your assets and liabilities so you can keep track of your progress to financial freedom.

The BIG Thank You

It was a month after the sale of Ray Signs to Signs UK that Ken found himself clearing out his desk. It had been a sad day, but the team were really happy with the backing they were to get from a national company and it opened up many new options for them to grow in their roles.

As he rummaged to the back of the drawer, Ken pulled out the business card he remembered all too well. He had not spoken to Brad since his crisis moment and like most men he had been rubbish at keeping in touch and letting Brad know how he had got on.

He looked at the card and thought that as the time difference was in his favour he would give him a call and let him know what had happened.

"Hi Brad, now I don't suppose you remember me but it's Ken from the UK, the guy with the sign company that was having trouble a few years ago." Ken was hopeful that Brad would remember.

"Of course I remember you, Ken. You in trouble again? If you didn't get help last time I am not going to tell you anything different this time."

Ken got the feeling that Brad had a bit of a short fuse with people who did not take his advice.

"No, no, that isn't what the call's about, Brad. I just wanted to let you know that I did it. I got myself a coach, dedicated myself to learning, and I have just sold my business for an amount that I can officially retire on. And I just wanted to say thank you, as in a way you made this happen." Ken started to well up, and the last few words only just came out.

"Well bugger me mate, that's awesome news, well done and congratulations. Tell me about what happened since I last spoke to you."

Ken spent the best part of an hour talking through what he had done and how his life had changed over the last five years. Brad was attentive and loved hearing the story, so Ken kept on going, thinking with a wry smile that now that he had sold the business he was not going to have to pay for the long overseas phone call.

"Well thanks for calling, Ken, I do appreciate it. It's amazing how many people ask for my advice then ignore it totally, so it's great when somebody uses it and gets the results they deserve."

Ken could sense that Brad was about to make his excuse to go.

"Just one thing before I go," Brad said. "One of the perks of constant learning is that you have a lot now to give to others. Make sure you help as many people as you can, just as your coach and I have done with you. Remember that giving to others is far more enjoyable than having for yourself and if you give some away you make room to receive more. Take care and if you are ever in Vegas do pop round for a beer."

Ken bade Brad a fond goodbye and went back to clearing his desk, thinking of how he might one day be able to help others on their rollercoaster ride to success.

Lesson 15
Gratitude leads to greatness

Gratitude has been part of human existence for thousands of years, from the sacrificial offerings to the gods, to prayers in church and specific days such as Thanksgiving, and presents at Christmas.

As we learnt in lesson 12, we are what our brains make us feel, and it is our neocortex which controls how we interpret our place in the universe.

Showing gratitude allows this part of the brain to feel that it has helped others and has a sense of being, but gratitude affects us deeper than that. The limbic system drives our emotional wants, of which one is relationships with others. Thus being grateful makes us feel at one with those around us as it stimulates this part of the brain as well. Finally, if we are feeling grateful then we are unlikely to be feeling threatened and thus it will have a calming influence on our reptilian brain.

All in all, being grateful is key to us feeling happy and content with our lives, but I am sure you will all agree that we do it too infrequently. The problem is that in the haste of our busy lives we neglect many of the basic laws of gratitude, and thus miss out entirely on their positive effects.

So here's a good refresher, for all of us:

1. Be grateful for what you have, and you'll end up having more. Focus on what you don't have, and you'll never have enough.

2. Being happy won't always make you grateful, but being grateful will always make you happy. It's nearly impossible to appreciate a moment and frown about it at the same time.

3. There's always something to be grateful for. You may have to look wider and deeper but you are alive and there are always people worse off so find one positive thing, no matter how small.

4. To be truly grateful, you must be truly present. It is no good living in the past or the future. Now is the only time you have control over.

5. A grateful mind never takes things for granted. The circumstance (or person) you take for granted today may not be there tomorrow.

I think that we put so much weight into trying to control every tiny aspect of our lives that we completely miss the forest for the trees. This is even truer if you own and run a business.

We must all learn from the past and plan for the future, but live in the present, so wherever your business rollercoaster takes you, learn to let go, relax a bit and ride the path that it takes you. If you BE and DO your best then you may HAVE what you want, but even if you don't, remember to be grateful for whatever it does bring you. In the words of Les Brown:

BIG Actions

1. Keep a gratitude log and write one thing down every day, without repeating yourself. It sounds hard but it will open your mind to what you really have.

2. Take every opportunity to speak to others about your journey: schools, networking groups, radio, etc. You only need to help one person to make it worthwhile.

3. Time is more important than money, so give yours unconditionally to those who love you, and it will come back to you.

– The End –

Or is it just the beginning of another ride?

Acknowledgements

There are so many people who could be in these pages. I feel that I have been blessed to meet so many people from whom I have learnt so much. So I am going to have to limit my thanks to a tiny few who have been key to making this book possible.

The first has to be my wife Jane, who has been with me every step of the way. From meeting her when I was 19 and we were studying for our accountancy exams together, to this day, she has encouraged me to go for my dreams.

Of course my mother and father Ken and Pam, to whom this book is dedicated. I just so wish I had got off my arse and written this sooner so they could have read it, and especially as, even if they thought it was rubbish, they would have told me it was great.

Then there is Brad Sugars, the guy who started ActionCOACH as his dream when he was 25 and turned it into the global organisation it is today.

To all the people who have employed me over the years, Alan and Colin Frampton for treating me as the brother from another mother, and of course Mr Shores, who will be smoking his pipe in heaven no doubt with some sarky comment on why he was not in the book.

To my book writing coach Karen Williams, who has spoken to me every week in order to help me through this rollercoaster of book writing and ensured that it is in your hands right now.

If your name is used as one of the characters in the book then you mean enough to me for me to put you in, and if it is not then it was just because I didn't have enough characters and I am grateful for you just being in my life.

Finally, thanks to all the authors who have provided inspiration to write this book and especially to those to whom I have referred to in the book itself. More information on them can be found at the following sites:

Malcolm Gladwell, *Outliers* – www.gladwell.com

Kevin Stansfield, *Profit Builders* – www.abc-solent.com

Robert Kyosaki, *Rich Dad Poor Dad* – www.richdad.com

Michael Gerber, *The E-myth Revisited*
– www.michaelegerbercompanies.com

Napoleon Hill, *Think and Grow Rich* – www.naphill.org

Rhonda Byrne, *The Secret* – www.thesecret.tv

Stephen Covey, *The Seven Habits of Highly Effective People*
– www.stephencovey.com

Jack Canfield, *The Success Principles*
– www.thesuccessprinciples.com

Noel Burch, *Four Stages for Learning* – www.gordontraining.com

Jim Rohn – www.jimrohn.com

Les Brown – www.lesbrown.com

About Kevin Stansfield

Born to Kenneth and Pamela Stansfield, sister of Lorraine, Kevin was brought up in a typical middle class family in Dover, Kent, England.

Schooled at state primary and secondary schools, Kevin was middle of the road when it came to his academic career. Choosing to follow in his father's footsteps into accountancy at the age of 18, he went to university, and then qualified in a firm that his father had once worked for. Kevin's life could have been set at an early age: good job, work the career ladder, become a partner, and retire with a pension, job DONE!

However, fate rather than goal setting and planning were to steer him in a direction that was most definitely not on the cards at the start.

Having spent nearly five years qualifying to become a chartered accountant, Kevin was congratulated by the senior partner with his P45, who told him the firm could not afford the pay rise that he would be seeking.

This bit of LUCK (!!!) led him to join a smaller accountancy firm just outside Southampton where he was to understudy the senior partner and replace him when he retired four years later. These were great years for Kevin, being mentored by an amazing man, Mr David Shores, who drove him hard but taught him so much.

The four years passed very quickly and at the age of 28 Kevin was ready to sign the partnership papers and commit to the firm for the rest of his life.

However, deep down Kevin knew this was not what he wanted. Without Mr Shores he would always be the junior partner, so seeing an opportunity with one of his clients, he jumped ship and started in industry with two brothers, Alan and Colin Frampton, and became their company's financial director.

Helping them take this business to a £4m turnover in four years was an amazing journey; again the lessons that were being learnt were to provide the basis for his future career. Unfortunately, that business was side-swiped by a supplier rationalisation programme that saw a team of 50 reduced to one in three months.

Undeterred, the three of them picked up the pieces and rebuilt the business, but Kevin had to find some additional work elsewhere as the business was no longer big enough to have a full-time FD.

Again chance was on his side because one of the companies involved with the failed business was expanding and they needed a part-time FD to help them with their acquisitions.

The next six years were spent building these companies into multi-million pound enterprises employing over 400 staff. Kevin had thoroughly enjoyed the ride, but now they needed a full-time FD and Kevin was not one to settle for the status quo.

Not knowing what he wanted to do next, he took the bold decision to take a year out and go back to university to do his Masters of Business Administration (MBA), the pinnacle of business education, or so he thought at the time.

Doing a two year course in nine months was no mean feat, and coming away with one of only two distinctions that year showed Kevin's determination to be the best he could at anything he tried.

With all of this practical and theoretical knowledge under his belt, Kevin was a little lost after the degree. Not wanting to be just another accountant, he could not decide in which direction he would go, but one thing was certain, he was going to build his own business.

Again fate had its hand, or, as Kevin now realises, his Reticular Activating System had been programmed to be on the lookout for certain opportunities. The opportunity it came across was ActionCOACH, the world's #1 business organisation that was starting out in the UK having come from Australia and the USA.

Being a keen sportsman, Kevin fully understood the power of coaching, and the realisation that if business was just a game, having a coach on your team would surely give you a better chance of success. Kevin bought into the franchise, which gave him access to some of the best training, systems and tools that are available, and began his business.

None of his friends understood why he would give up a good accountancy career and pay to buy a franchise. Only his wife Jane, his previous boss Mr Shores and his parents encouraged him to go with his heart.

Ten years later Kevin has built one of the most successful business coaching practices in the world. He is also one of the most awarded ActionCOACH in the world, which itself is the most awarded and successful coaching business.

Having helped over 200 businesses in and around Hampshire, Kevin is on a mission to help even more and build his team of coaches so that every business has the opportunity to work with a professionally trained coach that will help them achieve their goals.

Outside of work, Kevin – as you might guess – is a keen single figure handicap golfer. He plays competitive tennis, and is never more at home than at the wheel of a convertible sports car or on a powerful motorbike.

More can be found about Kevin and his firm at

www.abc-solent.com or email kevinstansfield@actioncoach.com.

How can we help YOU?

The starting point to answering this question is that having a coach is not for everybody and you do not need one to be successful or happy in your business. Just as you can play any sport without having been coached. Go to any sports club and you will find people perfectly happy playing their game. When you ask them why they aren't working each week with a coach, they will give you a funny look and ask why they would need one.

The truth is that if you are happy playing at the level you are then there is no need to improve. If all the people you play with are about your level, if you did improve then you would soon outgrow those people and have to look for new playing partners. Also the older you get the less inclined you are to change and learn new skills or push yourself to the next level.

If, on the other hand, you are a competitive person who loves pushing yourself in all areas of your life, or you happen to be in a business that is always changing and growing, then if you chose to stand still you will actually find yourself going backwards. Again think of the sports club, but this time think of a 12-year-old whose group of friends are getting better every week. If they do not keep up and improve themselves, they will actually get left behind and either fall down into the group behind or more likely quit the sport completely.

Coaching is only for those of us who want to move forward and see every day as a new challenge to overcome. To push the boundaries of our comfort zone and revel in the possibilities of being better.

Being coached is not plain sailing. A coach's job is threefold:

1. To help you set your goals and draw up your plan of action.

2. To educate you on the things you don't know you don't know.

3. To help you implement your plan, keep you focused and accountable, provide support and help when it is needed, and celebrate the successes with you.

Running a business can be one of the hardest and most lonely things you can do. It can also be one of the most exciting and rewarding things. The only certainty is that it will always be a rollercoaster ride and having somebody at your side to help you through the ups and downs will be one of the best investments you can make.

How to contact us:

www.abc-solent.com

(+44) 02380560833

kevinstansfield@actioncoach.com

Lightning Source UK Ltd.
Milton Keynes UK
UKOW01f0847300617
304366UK00002B/29/P

9 780995 739062